RE-DESIGN

BUSINESS MODELS OF THE FUTURE

Christopher Gibbons

Copyright 2013 All rights reserved

WHY READ THIS BOOK?..4
WHAT THE BOOK IS ABOUT..9
        DO YOU HAVE THE RIGHT BUSINESS MODEL?
....11
THE THREE PARTS TO THIS BOOK......................................14
        PART ONE: UNDERSTANDING WHERE WE ARE
....15
        PART TWO: THE FUTURE.......................................16
        PART THREE: THE RE:DESIGN CYCLE...............18
CHANGE IS IN THE AIR...20
TECHNOLOGIES PATH TO USEFULNESS........................22
USEFULNESS..26
        The Social Web:...27
        The Semantic Web:..28
        The Internet of Things:..29
        Artificial Intelligence:...29
SHARE-ABILITY...34
        Some interesting social media facts...........................37
GETTING A REALISTIC VIEW OF YOUR
PERFORMANCE... 42
DOES IT APPLY TO EVERY BUSINESS?............................45
COMPANIES THAT LEAVE IT TOO LATE.........................47
        Take the Yellow Pages as an example........................48
THREE SIGNS, ITS TIME TO RE:DESIGN..........................54
        Need I say more?..55
CUSTOMERS DON'T KNOW WHAT THEY WANT..........56
REVOLUTION NOT EVOLUTION..59
GETTING INSPIRED OR... STEALING................................66
GETTING THE JOB DONE..69
CREATE A RE:DESIGN HABBIT..76
PROTOTYPES, TESTING & LAUNCH..................................78
        Bullets and Cannonballs...80
HOW YOUR SALES, MARKETING AND DELIVERY
NEED TO ADAPT... 82
CUSTOMERS INCENTIVES FOR CHANGE.......................90
        SPEED AND CONSISTENCY..................................92
        PRICE..92

- LOCATION & ACCESSIBILITY...............92
- LOOK & FEEL.................94
- FEATURES OF YOUR NEW BUSINESS MODEL............95
  - FREEMIUM 96
  - ONDEMAND.................98
  - MOBILE..................100
  - SOCIAL & COMMUNITY.................102
  - END TO END...................104
- THE RE:DESIGN PROCESS...................107
- RE:DESIGN CYCLE.................110
  - RE:CALIBRATE.................112
    - WHO NEEDS A JOB DOING?.................113
    - WHAT JOB NEEDS DOING?.................113
    - WHY DOES THE JOB NEED DOING?.................113
  - CALIBRATION EXAMPLES:...................114
  - RE:DESIGN.................116
  - DESIGN EXAMPLES.................118
  - RE:CALCULATE.................119
    - OVERHEADS.................120
    - COST OF DELIVERY.................120
    - PROFIT TARGETS & BREAK EVEN.................121
    - BREAK EVEN CALCULATION.................122
  - RE:CONFIGURE.................123
    - MEASUREMENTS.................124
  - EXECUTION.................127
- It's just the beginning.................129
  - THINGS YOU MAY NEED.................130
  - AT LEAST TWO FULL DAYS:.................131
- ABOUT CHRIS.................132
- RESOURCES & RECOMMENDATIONS FOR INSPIRATION ON CUSTOMER EXPERIENCE RE:DESIGN 135

WHY READ THIS BOOK?

OUR BUSINESS MODELS ARE KILLING US.

Dinosaurs were instantly wiped off the face of the planet when a giant meteorite came crashing to earth. During the last five years innovations in technology have created the equivalent, 'game changing events' in business. If your business does not adapt it too will be wiped out.

There are some basic principles of life and business that always remain constant. Do your best, don't harm others etc. What changes over time is the availability of useful tools to help us apply these principles and in theory at least, make life easier, improve our efficiency and hopefully much more enjoyable.

For the last ten years my work has been about helping other people in business get closer to setting up their work around their life and *not* the other way round. I have met so many people in jobs they hate. Too many people are in businesses that are literately killing them with stress and exhaustion.

A few years ago I was running lots of regular workshops and seminars, mostly on the topic of sales and marketing for small and medium sized companies. In 2007 (ie. before the world entered a big recession and business became *really* tough) over the course of 12 months we had three business owners who were due to attend one of my programmes, cancel at the last minute. These cancellations were not because of additional work meetings, child care issues, car problems or any of the excuses I had expected. These people could not attend because they had been admitted to hospital with some kind of stress related issue. I always knew there were people out there having a hard time running their companies, but it's not till I came face to face with the impact of this that I realised how serious it can get. I always believed that running a business should be about freedom, this was not what I expected.

After spending a few years working on some business projects that did not really achieve what I intended, I found out how easy it might be to fall into this trap.

When I am focused on what I am good at, things seem easy. Sounds obvious but I know many business owners who don't seem to be enjoying their business. Part of the point of RE-DESIGNING your company is to make it a more enjoyable place to be and work. Designing a BUSINESS MODEL that supports your customers in the best way possible will by default also make it a more enjoyable and fun place to be.

When your BUSINESS MODEL is giving your customers the most amazing experience, to the point they absolutely love your business, then, your business will be much easier to run. You are likely to enjoy it more and because you are successful, its much more likely you'll have the resources to hire a team of people to do the things you do not want to do or are actually, *not that good at doing*.

On the other hand, if your business is mediocre at supporting customers, they are not raving about how good you are and you do not have a waiting list of people looking to work with you, then business can be pretty tough. This is obviously not an enjoyable experience and means many people dread getting up and going to the office in the morning.

There is a common thread among most management teams when discussing areas of their business they want to fix, improve or develop. It starts with something like... 'we need to improve our marketing, we need to cut our costs, our sales people need training, our IT systems are out of date, we need new suppliers...."

I have never met a business owner or management team who say,

> 'my customers are getting a really average service... we need to do a better job.'

It's very hard to admit, maybe hard to even spot in your own business. It usually takes a fresh set of honest eyes to see your customer experience for what it really is.

Who would even want to be associated with a business that was not serving it's customers well? It's especially hard to admit for most business owners, because essentially it's their fault. If you are a business owner and do *not* have a long list of people who are waiting to work with you, tell their friends about how good your business is, send you thank you messages because of how happy you have made them, then unfortunately you have a business that could do with some improvements to it's BUSINESS MODEL.

The more time invested in designing the system and structure behind how we serve our customers, how we deliver, how we package services and how we behave as a business, the simpler the more tactical areas of business become. When you have a great BUSINESS MODEL the tactical operations of sales, marketing, HR, finance and administration almost take care of themselves. Theses areas still require attention and expertise to be executed well, but, they are much more straight forward and run with a far greater degree of success. Most importantly this leads to a more enjoyable place to work, and to be a customer of.

When your company is delivering outstanding service to the point where people can't help but share the story of how you operate, lots of interesting things start to happen. Marketing becomes a case of just communicating to the people who have already found you, sales is more about *rationing* who you actually serve as customers (Thanks to David and Jonathan Holland for that line), and hiring your next superstar team member becomes obvious because you have a long list of people who want to be part of your business.

INTRODUCTION

WHAT THE BOOK IS ABOUT

We live in a time where new technology should have given us more freedom, fun, health and wealth, so why is it so many business owners and executives are working so hard, for often average financial results?

Management teams are repeatedly asked to find ever more innovative strategies that will;

- Increase sales...
- Boost profits...
- Find better employees.

These questions have been examined countless times by research papers, consultants and authors, so what is different about RE-DESIGN? Do we really need another book that tells us how important it is to, *go the extra mile*, *build a structured delivery system* or, *find a target market*? Not really.

When worked on individually these questions often focus our attention on treating the symptom, not the cause.

We all know that switching from eating full fat ice cream to a low fat ice cream is not really going to help us loose weight. The ice cream could just be one element of your diet. What about exercise? What about the sugary drinks? To get real lasting change an entire lifestyle change is required. In the same way investing more in a new marketing campaign or training our sales teams is unlikely to have any significant impact if our BUSINESS MODEL is not right to begin with.

I have seen many companies invest in improving their marketing strategy, training their sales team, changing their branding and dozens of other obvious tactical areas of their business all in the hope it will take their companies to the next level. Rarely do companies go right back to the start and examine their *BUSINESS MODELs*. *What job are you aiming to do, who do you want to do it for and how will you get it done*. This book asks precisely these questions.

DO YOU HAVE THE RIGHT BUSINESS MODEL?

When I talk about BUSINESS MODELs I am talking about the *way* we do business. Since 2006 no business book would be complete without a few comments and entries from Wikipedia.

Wikipedias entry on BUSINESS MODEL says,

> A BUSINESS MODEL describes the rationale of how an organization creates, delivers, and captures value[1] (economic, social, or other forms of value). The process of BUSINESS MODEL construction is part of business strategy.
>
> http://en.wikipedia.org/wiki/Business_model

Does anybody really understand what that means? This book is not designed to be more complex than necessary so I have a much more straight forward definition.

BUSINESS MODEL;

> WHAT JOB DO YOU DO, WHO FOR AND HOW?

In defining your own BUSINESS MODEL it's important to have a clear and detailed understanding of all three elements.

How your *BUSINESS MODEL* is defined should be very specific to your customer base. Ask an average hotelier, *what their BUSINESS MODEL was*, they'd tell you;

"We provide a bed and breakfast in return for a nightly fee"

The issue with this definition is that it could apply to any hotel. A boutique hotel that focused on attracting couples for short romantic breaks clearly needs a different *BUSINESS MODEL* to a hotel aimed at providing a *no-nonsense* service to business travelers.

The first two elements of defining your *BUSINESS MODEL* , 1) What job you do, 2) Who you do it for; are the foundations for designing, *How* you do it. A hotel may have the job of providing...

- ... a place to sleep at short notice for business travelers, or.
- ... a relaxing retreat for honeymooners.

Both these are completely different *jobs to be done* and require different *models* for delivery. The first, *a place to sleep at short notice for business travelers*, might focus on speed, accessibility and the availability of highly functional rooms. The last words you'd use to describe a, *relaxing retreat for honeymooners*, would be *speedy, accessible, available and functional*.

The usual starting point for designing or RE:DESIGNING a *BUSINESS MODEL* is to focus on the *How*. Sticking with the example of the hotel, this might include choosing locations, designing room layouts or restaurant menus. It's all too common for management teams to invest in *designing new BUSINESS MODELs*, packed with seemingly great features, with customer service systems that deliver brilliant experiences yet still not actually deliver a service that; *gets the job done*.

This book does cover the important changes in the world that impact *How*, your business, *gets the job done*, for your customers, but the first stage in your *BUSINESS MODEL RE:DESIGN* is to clearly define;

WHAT JOB YOU DO & WHO YOU DO IT FOR.

How you get your job done needs investigation because technology and the way we communicate changed more in the last ten years than in the previous one hundred years. The world have never adapted so suddenly and most businesses have some catching up to do. These innovations did not creep up on us. In the last five years the whole landscape of personal and business communication has adjusted and even most so called *experts* are still learning as they go.

This book is about understanding the impact of these changes on your business and RE:DESIGNING your BUSINESS MODEL so it can take advantage of our new landscape.

THE THREE PARTS TO THIS BOOK

PART ONE: UNDERSTANDING WHERE WE ARE

The first part of this book is to challenge business owners and management teams to create better models of doing business.

Improving your BUSINESS MODEL will impact the performance of every department in your company. But, before we get into the details of RE:DESIGNING your BUSINESS MODEL we need to understand our new landscape and how we got here. Understanding this means we can look at some of the reasons why a business RE:DESIGN should be on the cards for most of us.

All too often companies react to poor results by investing more in sales and marketing, or blaming the 'poor economic climate'. This books first job is to point out that if you want a better performing business then you *first* need to evaluate your model for doing business. If you want great performing sales and marketing campaigns, then build something, that's really easy to sell.

PART TWO: THE FUTURE

The second part to this book looks at how your future BUSINESS MODEL might look like.

Over the last ten years we have seen huge changes in the way we behave as customers, mainly due to how we use technology and in particular the internet. Think about how your own habits have changed.

Many 'big' businesses have adapted and improved their models to match our new demands as customers, yet most small and medium sized companies seem stuck. With our business environment having changed and continuing to change at such a fast pace most business people I speak to feel paralysed, not knowing what to work on first and in the end, doing nothing. Creating a better website, designing an mobile smart phone app, spreading the word using social media, creating an automated email marketing system, selling services online, outsourcing...there are just too many options to write down, let alone act on.

This book is for businesses who know they should adapt and are looking for some guidelines for taking the first step.

If you feel that your business is working perfectly and *there is no need* to look at adapting your BUSINESS MODEL, then don't stop reading just yet, this book could be for you too. You never know how you might feel after reading it. The world is changing so quickly that just when you feel like everything us under control, it all changes again. The process of RE:DESIGN is constant. It's a process that once you start should never be stopped, a bit like decorating your home. What looks good now, might need updating in a few years.

What impact have these global changes have already had on our lives and what are some of the most likely predictions for how this will effect the way we do business in the future.

I'll also talk about why very soon it will be almost impossible to run a successful business without customer service being at the core, how this will almost always lead to businesses being highly integrated with technology and how this will impact how all sales, marketing, service and product are delivered.

It could sound like a *cliché*, saying that customer service will be the central focus of the most successful businesses of the future. Hasn't this always been the case? Yes, but there are some very important facts that have entered our everyday life that mean unless customer service is truly your number one focus, you will get *'found out'* very quickly. Have you ever met a business owner who would admit that their customer service is poor? Yet we all know businesses with terrible service, so they do exist.

I do not believe this poor *service* is down to lack of effort or enthusiasm. In fact the vast majority of business people I meet are the most caring, generous and hard working people I have ever met. These businesses are usually just operating outdated BUSINESS MODELs that need updating or, RE:DESIGNING.

The core message of this book is that providing a great customer experience is no longer a good thing to do, it's a must. To achieve this we must build BUSINESS MODELs that is focus on doing a very specific and useful jobs for customers.

This means when designing your BUSINESS MODEL we need to examine everything from the way your business looks and feels, to how fast you actually deal with customers, to the services and products the customer might use in conjunction with yours, to your pricing model, to the technology you develop to deliver your products and your customer service systems.

PART THREE: THE RE:DESIGN CYCLE

You'll not be able to simply complete the questions and walk away with a new fine tuned BUSINESS MODEL... it will require work.

Think of the RE-DESIGN model as a guide to getting you started. It my belief that the process you go through to develop your new business model, the time you invest 'thinking about it', brainstorming with your team, suppliers and customers is far more important than the document you use to record it.

Every industry, customer base and business owner has totally different requirements. It's impossible to say what features your new BUSINESS MODEL must include, there are too many unrelated factors. What this books will give you is a structure for designing or RE:DESIGNING your BUSINESS MODEL.

This book to be short and to the point and designed to give an overview of many of the subjects. If you discover a particular topic of relevance then I strongly suggest further research. I have included a, *Resources* section at the back but don't let this limit you.

Weather you acquired this book purchasing on amazon, stealing from a book store, illegally downloading or borrowing the book from a friend, thank you for reading. I hope you find it useful.

THE SITUATION

CHANGE IS IN THE AIR.

In times of significant economic disruption consumers will actively seek new ways to get things done. In response, in 2010 a report by the *Federation of Small Business* suggested that as much a 68% of companies had innovated their services or products in the hope of combatting the economic downturn.

It's no secret that the world economy has been going through a hard time. Whatever your view, however it has or *has not* impacted your life, there is a general view taken by the press that, *business is tough* and, *we need to search for new solutions*. In fact the apparent shortage and scaling back of resources like *funding* have actually encouraged innovation in many industries. If your services and products are being delivered in the same way as they were 5 years ago *and* you have found the last few years in business challenging then, it's quite likely your business is running an out-dated *BUSINESS MODEL*. Is your BUSINESS MODEL designed to provide what consumers wanted five years ago or, has it adapted to provide for what they are looking for now?

The entire world economy and technological landscape has changed, in turn, so must your business. Before we look at exactly *what has changed in the world* that means a, *BUSINESS MODEL RE-DESIGN* is required, it's important to understand how we arrived in our new landscape.

TECHNOLOGIES PATH TO USEFULNESS.

Looking back to understand where we are heading....

Since it's introduction there is no doubt that motor transport has improved efficiency in moving goods and people around the world. It took a while before the vehicles we produced were actually useful.

Automobiles (or sorts) first started to appear as early as the 1700's. There was lots of hype and many people, mostly the very rich early adopters, jumped in right away and purchased a car, if only for the novelty factor.

This also reminds of my first *Smartphone*. Myself and other *early adopters*, got to experience the wonders of owning a *Windows Mobile Phone*, in about 2003. A great idea (just look at how the concept worked for the iPhone) but totally impractical, slow and unreliable.

Back to automobiles. In the 1800's roads were poor, vehicles were unreliable and expensive and finally not even quicker than using your traditional horse and cart. The automobile only really became useful after the industry started to produce highly specialised versions of their vehicles to suit different tasks - transporting people, light goods, heavy goods, farming vehicles.

The same process is happening right now with Electric Car. The electric car has been around as a concept for over 20 years but till recently it has been totally useless. It is only in recent years that we have had the technology to get a useful balance between the efficient use of the technology and affordability. In the same way the internet is only just starting to become useful too.

So, after a technology is introduced it takes a number of years of trail and error to understand how it will best be made useful.

When talking about this topic most people can see straight away how it applies to the Electric Car, when I start talking about this being the case with the internet I get a mixture of worried and confused looks.

"but i just invested $25,000 in my new website! What do you mean it's not useful"

Most people are very defensive about their own websites, but very few websites, especially in the small and medium sized business sectors actually contribute anything significant to the company BUSINESS MODEL. Most websites are used as on-line sales literature. There is nothing *wrong* with this, in fact on-line sales literature has been one of the best used of the internet and webpages. But, now technology allows us far more uses.

The internet and the technology it enables us to incorporate into our BUSINESS MODELs is so powerful that it can almost always improve how we deliver our services and products. Not taking advantage of this is a little but like hiring Gordon Ramsey to cook you egg on toast. I am sure he would do a great job, but it's hardly putting his talent to good use.

Many of the worlds business leaders, remain in the dark when it comes to technology.

I am not talking about large corporates or small technology startups... I am talking about the rest of us. Think about your hairdresser, your local hospital, printing company, building firm or any other small or medium sized firm. How many of them would you say are leading the way with a technology enabled integrated BUSINESS MODEL? Very few is my guess. Thats the exciting thing. This gives us much opportunity for improvement!

Generation Y (people born between about 1981 -1991), is expecting more and more from the services available to them online. In the main, they do not have technical skills and expect their computer software to be user-friendly and to coin an over used Apple marketing line, *just work*. Generation Y have been exclusively brought up using computers and software that was reliable and useful. We often hear people talk about, *how smart,* young people are with computers. In fact the generation with the most understanding of what makes a computer system work are now almost all thirty plus. Generation Y or the under thirties, have new expectations.

The internet is beginning to mature into it's early twenties years, but only just. Just like all twenty years olds, it's just starting to become useful. We'll discuss more on exactly how it's becoming useful later, but the important thing about usefulness is that it's closely linked with value.

If you think the internet has created wealth now, then wait and see what then next twenty years bring. Until recently everything created using internet technology has been innovated using unreliable, slow and expensive technology. The drive in technology improvements as been led by the need to power our complex software, but now we have reached a point where our technology can run our most complex software with capacity spare. Remember the time when your computer would take ten minutes just to *boot up* or it would take 5 hours to download a song from Napster? Yet, just yesterday afternoon I was able to watch a live tennis match on my iPhone while waiting for a train. Technology has improved so dramatically it's hard to remember a time without it.

USEFULNESS

The first consumer versions of what we would recognise as the *internet* emerged in the early nineties and would later be described as Web 1.0. Then we had what became known as Web 2.0 and now we have moved into stage three or Web 3.0.

The internet pre 2000 was mostly about publishing. Publishing your company profile, sales information or product descriptions, effectively an online sales brochure. There were a limited number of online shops but most were basic and in the very early stages of acceptance among the average consumer.

The mainstream introduction of what became known a Web 2.0 occurred between 2000-2010. Web 2.0 gave users the chance to interact with the websites they used, to publish their own content and to create social networks. Essentially Web 2.0 was still about publishing, but it allowed everyday users to actually become authors of their own content.

Web 3.0 has been described as *The Transcendent Web*, in a interesting report by, Booz&Co. This report is available on their website, www.booz.com.

The Transcendent Web means an internet experience that goes beyond publishing or consuming content. Web 3.0 is about the internet becoming a useful and perhaps integrated part of our lives.

According to Booz&Co, Web 3.0 contains four key elements. The Social Web, The Semantic Web, The Internet of Things and Artificial Intelligence.

The Social Web:

The recent developments in internet technology mean a third major shift in how we are able to communicate. If you like a *COMMUNICATION 3.0*.

1.0 : One to one conversations. When we, the human race first invented language and began to have discussion it was only possible on a one to one basis or in very small groups (hearing distance).

2.0 : One to many conversations. With technology innovations came the printing press and eventually radio and television. This gave us the power to create a message once and broadcast it to thousands if not millions of people.

3.0 : Many to many conversations. The internet is the first media that allows us not only create and broadcast a message, but also to receive a response. To conduct an interactive conversation with our audience. The second important feature of *many to many* conversations is that consumers also become publishers. It's this important distinction that also changes how our BUSINESS MODELs operate.

As a business it's becoming increasingly more difficult to control what messages, either good or bad, are broadcast about your company. With our new ability to become publishers of content it's your consumers who get the most attention when it comes to, *what is said about you*. This is an important change and one that needs embedding into your *BUSINESS MODEL RE:DESIGN*.

The Semantic Web:

First described by Tim Bernards-Lee, inventor of the World Wide Web, The Semantic Web describes how the availability of internet users personal preferences gives us a data source that will create a highly personal internet experience. We are already seeing sites such as Facebook, uses this data for advertising. Adverts are displayed to highly targeted user groups based on information contained within their user profile.

The Internet of Things:

Soon, the time will come when your fridge, vacuum cleaner and dishwasher are all able to communicate to you and each other over the internet. *The Internet of Things* means that our electrical devices will be able to be controlled remotely over the internet. Why is this useful? Well apart from the novelty of being able to switch on the vacuum cleaner while you are out at the beach (or something similar) there are many ways in which devices can use their connectivity to improve their energy efficiency. Your devices will "*talk*" to other devices on your local power grid, using the data to know when to switch themselves on and off at the most efficient time. Another example might be that your printer automatically orders a new ink when it's running low. Your fridge lets you know when the milk is '*off*' and makes sure you get a fresh bottle in your next home delivery.

Some of these systems are already up and running, others have some way to go and will take maybe another ten years before they are fully integrated into our lives.

Artificial Intelligence:

This is where the internet starts to get really useful. Using software based decision making tools some routine tasks will be taken over by invisible online solutions. This will mean our search engines will not only be personal but may also be able to predict what we need, before we need it.
Imagine being in a supermarket looking through ingredients and discovering a rare vegetable. You like the look of it but have no idea what to use it with. Without a keyboard, mouse or voice command you simply pick up the vegetable and out of thin air an image appears next to this new strange looking vegetable. The image might give you some nutritional information and display a list recipe ideas.

This technology is already in development. Google and a few other research firms are doing brilliant work in bringing this, *Augmented Reality,* technology to the point where it's accessible to us all.

We are a few years away from some of the examples above, but already some of this technology is being integrated into our lives. As a quick example, and because I think it's really cool, let me tell you about a new App for my iPhone.

I have been using a computer for diary management for about 10 years, and it's only just got to the point where it's much better than a pen and paper. Maybe thats an exaggeration, but it's not far from the truth.

When I started using a computer for diary management I had some software that sat on my computers hard drive. If I was away from my desk I had no idea what was written in it. In about 2003, I was able to start syncing my Windows phone with my calendar. This gave me a mobile version of my diary. When I came back to the office (*and if I remembered and the software actually worked*), I would plug it in and, hey presto, both my computer and my phone were *synced*. This system was actually starting to get useful for geeky or if that is impolite, computer literate people, but for the average user this system was far to unreliable. Most people I knew *synced* their devices for the first 2-6 weeks of ownership, then just got fed up with the whole process.

When I moved to an iPhone in 2007, I started storing my diary online. My phone and my computer would all sync into the '*cloud*' and I'd always have an up to date version of my diary. The '*cloud*', if you do not already know is a term used to describe some kind of computer storage that sits outside your own network. Imagine a hard drive that you can access from anywhere in the world. To me this new cloud based syncing service was great because it allowed my assistant to access exactly the same data as me, even when I was out of the office. We used it

to change or add meetings to my calendar while I was out of the office and all the details would automatically updated.
Next came the really clever innovation...

The latest version of my diary goes a little further. It now knows where I am. If I get a call from a friend while in a meeting I can now tap a button and have my phone remind me to call - when I leave the meeting. If I know I need to pickup some new printer ink while I am next in the area of printing shop I can tell my phone, next time I am near the shop, remind me to go in and get some.

Yes, I know this is a bit geeky, but it's actually really useful.

The internet and the services it creates has lots more data about me and my habits it can start to help me. It becomes a useful tool. Until now the internet has only allowed me to publish data, and do things when I specifically ask it to. Web 3.0 follows you round and can integrate with your life by performing some things for you. A bit scary, a bit Orwellian? Maybe. This is maybe not the best example of how this technology can be used, but it's a start. There are far more interesting a useful applications for this new availability of interactive data.

Having the ability for customers interact with data changes how we as businesses can deliver our services.

Amazon.com is a another great example. They use our previous buying decisions and history of other customers buying decisions to make personal recommendation to us, I am sure you have seen their, *"People who brought this also brought..."* section. They have also now made an app that lets you order products on the move. There is even a mobile app with a built in bar code reader that allows users to scan the code of product in a store. The app then delivers a list of all the places it can find the product you scanned, tells you how much it is, provides user reviews and also an, 'order now' button.

Technology like this is changing all our businesses and the way we make purchasing decisions. Already there are many services that most of us would only access on some kind of mobile device. Music, video, directory services have been available for a relatively long time (at least in the technology world), now other industries are catching up.

You may not yet be in a business that has vast quantities of useful data or even have the ability to allow your customers to interact with you using internet applications, but soon this will make you a minority. We have seen big companies start to incorporate these technologies into their business. What happens in big companies always flows into small and medium sized businesses.

I recently interviewed Jeffery Gitomer (Author of more than ten best selling books on business, sales and marketing, www.buygitomer.com) for a business show I host on, The Business Journal Online (www.thebusinessjournalonline.com). Jeffery says that,

> "Unless your business is able to serve it's customers when they want and how they want, 24/7, 365 you'll soon be dead. Integrating with technology is no longer an option."

We have just gone through a long period of technology innovation but this *technology* is only just finding it's usefulness in the world. This is really key in looking at designing your next BUSINESS MODEL.

Later in this book we will look at how even the most hands on and traditional industries are changing their BUSINESS MODELs to adapt to our new expectations as customers. There are some examples of taxi operators, printing firms, and even hospitals. All of these industries require hands-on, face to face, person to person contact to deliver their product or service to their customers. The core of what the company does usually remains the same, however, the way the products and services are delivered has adapted to include technology, improving the experience of both customers and workers.

SHARE-ABILITY

Most of us would make great amateur detectives. Facebook, LinkedIn or even Google have given the world a platform for sharing their most personal details. There is no point in denying, we have all done a quick background check on a person we are about to meet, it's now incredibly easy to do so. Find their Facebook page, examine their work history on LinkedIn or see if they appear on YouTube... it's not easy to stay anonymous. And worse, if you are anonymous then it leads to a bigger question, why? Being found online, especially in business is part the first stage of showing credibility for most people.

Of course the same is true about your business. You must be *searchable*. Many would argue that unless you appear on Googles first page of search results for key words relevant to your business then it's likely you'll not be in business very long.

We are now at the point where most consumer focused industries have at least one or two full google page of search results dedicated to providing reviews, blogs, ratings and gossip on how companies in their sector are performing.

Some industries are yet to catch up. One of my clients is in the Electronic Cable Assembly industry, and most websites and comments in this domain are not that well read and actually hard to find... but we predict it will not be long before this changes for them too. If your industry is not subject to full scale user reviews, it soon will be.

But most of us already know this. We spend thousands on building great websites and engaging search engine optimization practices. There is another key to making use of internet technology that must be incorporated into your *BUSINESS MODEL Re:Design*.

The key change between controlling your online image now and controlling it 5 years ago is that now, you are no longer directly in control of what is posted online. It's really important to have a great website, social media profile etc. It's far more important to get people talking positively about you.

Someone once taught me a valuable lesson in sales. If you say something good about yourself, then your prospect will look for a way to prove you wrong, if someone else says something positive about you, then it gets almost instant credibility. The most obvious proof of this in action is to consider you own buying decisions. When a *salesman* last told you that his product was the fastest, cheapest or best on the market, did you a) take his word for it or b) do some quick research online?

Sharing has become the number one use of the internet and since 2011 social media sites had more pages visits than any other category.

Some interesting social media facts...

- 50% of mobile internet traffic is social media.

- 34% of users share customer service experiences

- 1 in 5 hetrosexual and 2 in 5 gay marriages begin on social media platforms.

- Justin Bieber has more followers than the entire population of Greece, Australia and Sweden.

This is not a book about the *social media* revolution. This topic has been covered enough times in other books. However what is still very much misunderstood is how the *sharing* revolution will impact our *BUSINESS MODELs*. At this point in time we have a handful for companies leading the way with great social media driven marketing machines. Companies like GroupOn grew faster than any other business in history, yet the majority of businesses are yet to complete the profile page on their Facebook account. There are a tiny percentage of companies that have actually started to incorporate our new *culture of sharing* into their BUSINESS MODELs, yet I have not met a single CEO who believes it will not effect their industry. There are larger group of businesses who have put a toe in the water but setting up accounts with major *social media* services and maybe they even send an update a few times a week. Far fewer organizations are actually using these services in useful or engaging way.

Yo Sushi, a international chain of funky sushi restaurants re-slow mid-week period. Late of afternoon my partner received an update from *Yo Sushi* telling her that the first 1000 people to *checkin* at their restaurants would receive a free meal. In case you have been living in a box for the last five years, *checking in*, means clicking a button on your Facebook account that tells the world where you are.

We made it into the first 1000 and sure enough we got our free meal. This campaign was one of the best examples I have seen of interactive and *social* marketing. It worked on so many level.

1) It was exciting enough to be shared. A free meal offer was unusual, Many companies offer discounted meals, but *FREE* is a novelty. Just from our own point of view, we shared the offer from *Yo Sushi* with all our friends, even before we *checkin*.

2) It had *shareability* built in. To make the offer work it had to be worth talking about, but this offer was so clever to access it you were forced into sharing. Nobody likes to be forced into sharing, but the reward was high enough.

3) The limited number of *winners* gave the offer a kind of game like dynamic. Do we leave the house and enter the race for the *free meal*? It was fun to be part of race.

I know this offer is often repeated and now run by other restaurants too because of how well it engages the audience. We have only managed to collect a free meal once in my household, but we enjoy playing the game every time.

The final point to make about this campaign is about how efficiently it reaches vast numbers of people. The average Facebook user has about 100 friends so, even if you only include the thousand people that actually managed to claim a free meal that still one hundred thousand people. In actual fact many more people *checkin* hoping to claim a free meal so this number could be much higher.

An even better advantage to this form of marketing in comparison to traditional display or print advertising is of how well it is targeted. Our social networks are a reflection of the people we like to be friends with, at its usual for our us to be friends with people who like the same things we like. It's not very often we are friends with people we have nothing in common with. This means that when businesses create messages that are shared they audience they are shared with is likely to be highly targeted.

Many of our internally generated marketing campaigns are wasted on finding ways to tell the world about, *how good we are*. If we accept that it's our customers *word of mouth* recommendations that will have the biggest impact on our future *BUSINESS MODELs* and not what *we* say then we must also adapt how we invest in marketing.

Your new *BUSINESS MODEL* must be worth talking about and where possible provide a platform that allows people to talk about it.

THE PROBLEM
THE FIRST STEPS TO CHANGE...

There are two challenges we must address before we begin to think about how to create a *BUSINESS MODEL* that delivers super happy customers who get efficient, useful and integrated services and products.

- Knowing where you are.
- Knowing where you need to be.

Most companies have an unrealistic picture of how they are perceived and think they are doing a better job than they really are. *Knowing where you are,* means getting a realistic picture of exactly how well you are currently performing. *Knowing where you need to be,* means understanding what your business should or could be doing to serve it's customers. Most customers do not even know what they want, so it's not an easy job.

GETTING A REALISTIC VIEW OF YOUR PERFORMANCE

Alcoholics Anonymous (AA) has a famous 12-step program to recovery that begins with members accepting that;

> The first step to recovery is admitting you have a problem.

The first step to *RE:DESIGNING* your BUSINESS MODEL is the same.

It's hard to write this chapter without sounding derogatory and insulting, so forgive me. Most people think their companies are doing a much better job at serving customers and delivering a *great experience* than they truly are. When having this conversation with management teams, most jump straight into comparing themselves with the competition.

> Hey, we do an amazing job for our customers! You should see how the company across town treats their customers, out customers love us!

All this could be true, but also totally irrelevant. Comparing yourself to the competition or industry standards is only a good idea if your comparison *BUSINESS MODELs* are any good.

Consider the candlestick maker. You could have been the worlds best, had efficient streamlined manufacturing process, a great market reputation and cash in the bank. When Edison finally cracked the design behind the lightbulb your existing way of doing business would fall apart. We don't need to go back as far as the electric light to discover similar industry shifts. Travel agents, Compact Disk manufacturers, music stores, local telephone directories, fax machine manufacturers, the list is endless.

The industry change does not always need to be about a significant technology innovation. Amazon created the biggest retail business in the world by making the online buying experience simple. There were e-commerce businesses before *Amazon* that had the same technology available but were unable to execute as effectively. **James Dyson** innovated the vacuum cleaner, making it *bag-less* and efficient. **Innocent Smoothies** created a whole new category of fruit drinks.

Most of us understand how quickly *things can change*, and how fast new companies can get off the ground. The existing companies in your sector are not the ones to watch... it's the businesses you have not even heard of yet.

Rather than building your model around the idea of improving the industry standards, aim to design something from scratch. Without the constraints of what already exists. More on this later, but it's important to acknowledge that, *you have some improvements to make*, before moving to the next step of *RE:DESIGNING*.

DOES IT APPLY TO EVERY BUSINESS?

Me: "Yes"

Company management teams:
"Ahh, but our business is different because...

Nope, your industry is not immune to change.

Of course it applies to your business... I think that covers it.

COMPANIES THAT LEAVE IT TOO LATE

You only have to look back over the last few years to find lists upon lists of companies who seemed to have everything going for them, great growth and thriving BUSINESS MODELs only to within a matter of a few months see them crash and burn.

Take the Yellow Pages as an example.

Can you remember a time, *not really that long ago*, when if you had a business then there was a 90% chance you could be found in the yellow pages. 90% might be an exaggeration, but very few companies did not advertise in the Yellow Pages. Some people will even remember some TV and Radio advertisements stating, *Find us in the Yellow Pages*, instead of announcing their contact details.

Put yourself in the position of being Yellow Pages. What possible threats could you see coming? Considering the strength of the brand and not to mention that fact that they already had most businesses as customers, its almost impossible to imagine a downfall.

Even when Yellow Pages saw Google coming they thought that because of their existing business they would be able to deal with this *small startup*. They eventually decided to setup yell.com, this did get some traction. They have managed to change the business focus, but, seem to be finding things fairly hard. Their revenues are down to about 65% of what they were only three years ago (2398m 2009 to 1580m 2012 approx. as results are not yet confirmed). They have invested in setting up other businesses that seem to be growing but these are service based offerings such as web design and online advertising and have nowhere close to the success of their core print advertising business.

I cannot tell you how to fight back if your industry has already been innovated, disrupted or improved (depending on your outlook). Sometimes, like Yellow Pages it's better to know when to *RE:DESIGN*. Yellow Pages did not attempt (at least for very long) and continue to sell us Yellow Pages adverts (I know this business still exists but it's not the focus of the company), they did not try to compete with the technology that was disrupting their industry, they focused instead on a changed their offering. They continued to focus on helping their core customers market, but the way they did that was totally different from their previous model.

The most common excuses I hear for not getting started on a *BUSINESS MODEL RE:DESIGN* are...

- I have time, things are steady in my industry.
- Nobody else is making changes.
- I am in an hands on business, this won't effect me.
- I don't have time.

Have you ever had an idea for a product or business and never taken action, only to find a few months or years later the idea became big business? I bet you have. I swear that **NetFlicks**, **LoveFilm** and **rightmove.co.uk** were all my idea. Of course the idea is never enough.

I can almost guarantee that someone in your industry is working on a new BUSINESS MODEL that they believe will be, *'the next big thing'*. If you are not one of these people then you run the risk of getting left behind.

The biggest reason to act now is that because these new BUSINESS MODELs are potentially so disruptive to your industry you should make sure you are at the very least ready to adapt. This means making sure that even if you do not get to the stage of executing your plans for your new *BUSINESS MODEL*, you should be aware of what your options are. Then, if you find yourself in a situation where you must act, you can.

I have some friends that run an Accounting firm that in the words of co-founder Lucy Cohen, "*is working on taking over the world*".

Sophie Hughes and Lucy Cohen run a fast growing Accounting firm that focuses on the self-employed and small business market. They have stripped back all of the unnecessary features of a traditional Accountancy firm, made it possible to access all your important financial data remotely and still get personal support when you need it. Their company is called **Mazuma Money** (Google it) and their main offering is a service that means all you need to do once a month is bung all your payment receipts and invoices into an envelope (They also provide the envelope) and they do the rest. Everything is trackable so you can see their progress on your book-keeping and within about a day you can access all your monthly reports and statements.

They have built the service to be highly efficient and their average team member copes with about 4 times the amount of clients the average accountant handles. They do all this and still have much stronger client relationships, loyalty and satisfaction than any other Accounting firm I have ever seen.

The point about **Mazuma** is that it is a still small and growing business of less than 50 people, but now they are on a role, have a brilliant system and great reputation. Other accounting firms that operate in this market are finding it very hard to come up with a better solution. If everything goes well for **Mazuma** over the next few years I predict they will be market leaders.

What would happen if someone came into your industry with a totally disruptive service?

If they found a way to deliver exactly what customers wanted at a much lower price point, in a much more convenient way...

How quickly could you change your offering to align with theirs?

Would this be quick enough?

I ask the *'what would happen if?'* question, but really it should be *'what will happen when?'*. Someone will eventually create a new way of doing business in your sector and your challenge is either be that person or be ready with the tools to catch up quickly.

Of course this is not a new danger to be aware of in business, there have always been people who innovate the way business is done. But, there has never been a time in which an industry could be changed so quickly. My advice is start work on this now, get ready and, if you can, act first.

Rather than take action, many businesses seems to fighting change. Maybe hoping they can protect their business model.

It's am impossible task. Things will change. But this does not mean being reckless and making innovations for innovations sake. Take your time and be well prepared with all your design, planning and execution of your new model.

In 2011 low cost carrier **Southwest Airlines** decided to announce a *BUSINESS MODEL* innovation that resulted in an estimated one billion dollar hit to their bottom line. After talking to their customers and conducting *market research* it was decided that what customers really wanted was to checkin their luggage at no additional cost. Anyone that has travelled on a low cost airline will know that it's common practice to be charged an additional for each bag checked in. On the surface this sounds like a great idea and something that customers would really appreciate. The innovation was made on the basis that because fairs would be lower, more customers would flock to the service. However, Southwests customer base remained steady.

It transpired that customers were actually not that interested in saving on checking in luggage. The key factor when choosing an airline was the ticket price. In the case of the low cost airline model the price of ticket was the key a feature. Customer may have declared that, *luggage fees* were an issue, but, even the customer is not always right.

In the case of **Southwest Airlines,** the innovation in *BUSINESS MODEL* was made on a part of their business that had little impact on how customers used the service. Sure, it was a great idea and no customer would complain about this *kind offer*, but at the same time they were not impressed by it.

When you do decide to launch a new model please make sure that before you release anything to your existing customers, abandon your current way of doing business or announce your own industry revolution, you have some proof that your new systems work and people like them.

It could even be worth testing your ideas under a totally different brand. More in this in the PROTOTYPE, TESTING & LAUNCH chapter.

THREE SIGNS, ITS TIME TO RE:DESIGN

Need I say more?

If you have got this far, then you'll have a good idea of why you should be looking at a RE:DESIGN. Everything around you is changing, change is the one constant.

CUSTOMERS DON'T KNOW WHAT THEY WANT

Ten years ago if you conducted some *market research* and asked consumers what they wanted in a new PC, the last thing they would have suggested is;

- less features.
- a closed user interface.
- a higher price tag.
- limited availability of software.
- poor compatibility with my existing setup.

Yet look at the success of Apple Mac Books and iMacs. These computer systems met serious criticism from PC users when first introduced. While they looked great many found the limitations imposed by Apples, *closed system* principles too much to take. It was not till users actually started reporting how these new devices were a *dream to live with* that people started to take note.

Computer users would never have considered asking for a *closed system* like the one Apple delivered, because they were unable to link this with benefits it actually provided.

It is not your customers job to spend their time trying to construct the perfect product or service, most customers do not even take the time to complain when something is bad... even when you ask very few will give your enough insights to design a new product. Creating this service is your job and it's one of your most important.

Some people suggest investing in market research. Ask customers what they want, then build it. The biggest challenge with this is that customers often do not know what they want. What I mean is that they have not really invested any significant, *thinking time*, into working out what they want.

Think about the last time you went to your local supermarket. There is a high chance you were not walking around thinking,

> "I like this place but I would really like it better if it had a bag packing service"

EVEN if you were asked to complete a customer survey that asked...

> What changes would you like to see in store?

Most people would have left the box blank.

Yet, if your store started offering a *bag packing service*, that took your bags to your car, packed them away... most of us would love it!

A *bag packing service* in a supermarket might not be the most inspiring of ideas, but thats not the point. It's a great example of an additional service that shoppers would be unlikely to suggest if asked in a *customer survey*, but if this service was in place, most would love it.

To come up with a great customer service experience doing *market research* is unlikely to lead to a revolution. Of course there will always be exceptions, but on the whole, if you put enough time and thought into your BUSINESS MODEL RE:DESIGN then you'll find you probably already have the answers.

REVOLUTION NOT EVOLUTION

RE:DESIGNING your new *BUSINESS MODEL* by innovating your existing *model* is often the most obvious place to start. It could also be the most worst place to start.

A useful story to remind ourselves of here is of the invention of the *'Space Pen'*, a pen that can be used in zero gravity. The story goes that the American space agency NASA spent millions upon millions of dollars trying to find a pen that would write in zero gravity. The Russians, used a pencil.

While this story is actually just urban legend it does make a useful point.

Rather than starting your RE:DESIGN project by adapting what you have, imagine you were starting again. What job are you trying to achieve? How would your customers like it done? What tools could you use?

When starting work on this process most people jump straight to looking at their existing BUSINESS MODEL, or the standard model for doing business in their industry and start looking for areas to improve. This is challenging because it assumes that the original BUSINESS MODEL is a good one.

Don't get me wrong, I am not saying that the way you do business now is not the best way to do business in the future, it's just that we cannot say for sure that this is the case.

When the average consumer first started using the internet it was mainly for basic communication (emails, instant messaging services etc) or research. You might have looked for some product reviews, check out the latest album by your favorite band or check what movies were showing at the cinema. In the main these sites were produced by professionals who also had print based publications. The more adventurous internet users would also sometimes make purchases online and even book a flight for their next holiday.

As bandwidth improved and consumer trust increased we moved into a more interactive phase, Web 2.0. Apart from the obvious communication services like GoogleMail, Skype and Facebook we also started to us the internet as software.

Rather than download Microsoft Word you could create all your documents in the cloud using GoogleDocs. In business many firms migrated away from using software installed on their own servers and used online packages such as SalesForce. This migration is still very much underway, with the vast majority still in the process of switching, or not quite convinced.

It's easy to see why some companies have not yet made the move. A few years ago these packages were just not good enough to use for commercial purposes. A few firms did make a switch, but most faced huge challenges incorporating these systems into efficient use. Even though there has been a shift in how we access these software packages, they have essentially not changed much. We are still required to sit at a desk or notebook and get the work done. The fact that the software sits on a computer that is no longer on our local machine does not really save us much time. The real revolution is coming from services that take away our old way of doing things. Services that *become much more useful than the old way of working*. The reasons I am so interested in this is because businesses too can build there products and services around the same idea. Become useful.

The whole purpose of technology is to improve efficiency and make our lives easier. The internet has done that to a certain extent but why is it that most people still work as hard as they did before.

While the internet software, websites, mobile applications can be helpful and more secure they rarely actually save us that much time. Of course I am talking very generally. There are some brilliant exceptions to this and some companies are doing a brilliant job. In the main they are few and far between.

Just taking the example of GoogleDocs. I really love the idea of being able to work on a document from any device or location, being able to collaborate with other users on the same document and having a secure backup of all my work stored in the cloud.

I was an early adopter of GoogleDocs, as I unfortunately am with most things. Thinking back over my time as a user I actually think it has taken up more of my time than if I used traditional software to perform the same tasks. I actually think I could have even been faster if I used a pen and paper.

> POSTSCRIPT: I am even editing this document and writing this very comment with a pen after printing the first draft... just proves my point.

Why? Well in my case, I am sure similar to the experience of others, it a number of reasons.

First, Googles software while very good was not the same as I was used to (MS Office). There were some tasks that I needed to re-learn and others that I just could not perform. This often led to me starting a document in Google, then having to download it into MS Office to finish it. It's not that the core product did not do what I wanted, it's just I knew that if I had used my *old* software I could get an additional feature. In reality these missing features were not essential to *getting my job done*, but because I knew they were missing I ended up spending hours trying to create work arounds. It's not that the software is bad, it's that I needed to relearn how to get the job done.

Let's look at another example. CRM or Customer Relationship Management (software used for managing your contacts diary and communications with prospects and customers). In the company I was with about 10 years ago I was considered the CRM Guru. I spent months traveling the country, on the telephone and at computers setting up, training the team and fixing the database tool designed to make the life of each of the consultants easier. It was not doing a great job and mostly confused people. The company embarked on investing $1,000,000 in designing it's own web-based CRM package... after 18 months this was abandoned and they invested another $300,000 in having an existing CRM package (SugarCRM) customised and rolled out round the world. This too was eventually abandoned and now most people in the company use a basic address book, spreadsheet and maybe some kind of dedicated mass email software.

The point is that all these solutions sounded like a great idea and brilliant timesavers. In reality they ended up being over complex and confusing to the average user. The most successful offices in the group often kept track of their sales and clients using a simple spreadsheet and whiteboard.

Both these are examples of software *evolution* not software *revolution*. RE:DESIGNING your BUSINESS MODEL should be more than making some *improvements* to how it already works. Like with these software *improvements*, sometimes businesses embark on using new technology to *add features* to their service. The issue is that often this actually distracts, not adds to service. Over featured and complex BUSINESS MODELs just make your service more difficult to explain, market and sell.

RE:DESIGNING your *BUSINESS MODEL* is most effective when *designed* from the ground up. This does not mean that your existing model should be abandoned. It means to effectively design a new model, it's easier done by starting with a *blank sheet*. This will free you from any limitations imposed by your existing ways of getting the *job* done.

Take the music industry as another example. The last ten years have been rocky to say the least. Big industry giants have been struggling to protect their old model of selling singles and albums from websites such as thepiratebay.org. These sites offer links to download almost anything for free. We all know the stories of legal battles, artists complaints and never-ending struggle of the '*pirates*' who attempt to avoid large *fines* and even stay out of prison. But there seems to be a solution emerging.

Services like Spotify are really starting to gain marketshare and as their coverage improves their new model for business seems much more appealing and acceptable. Spotify is a online subscription service that allows you to remotely access almost any music you wish, instantly. Spotify partners with most major record labels and pays them a small fee every time one of their songs is played, a bit like a radio station would pay a fee every time it plays a track. Users get the benefit of only paying a monthly subscription for listening to as much music as they like. Spotify is such a great example of industry innovation. At first this small startup had the record companies running in fear, until it got to the point where now ten million users are logging in to listen. Spotify and similar companies now hold the power in this industry. All this has happened since 2008 when they launched, (at the point of writing this), only four years ago.

If the whole music industry can be turned upside down in such a short space of time, then so can your industry.

So, why has it taken a small European tech startup, with little resources and a crazy idea like unlimited music downloads to change the industry. Surely big industry giants like Sony EMI have got more than enough resources to invest in creating and testing new models for doing business. It seems not. Now it looks as if they will find it hard to recover and find a place in a future industry.

It's not that Sony EMI or other music industry corporates did not try to adapt, they were not radical enough to go the whole hog, consider what their customers actually wanted and find a way to deliver it. Instead they focused on how they could adapt their existing model to fit in with a new world.

This may work for a period of time, but there will always be a battle. On one side you have the customers who are not really happy, because they know there is a better alternative and it's being kept from them. On the other side you have the companies who always feel like they are fighting a battle to protect themselves from what they may consider theft of their property.

Even if the company wins a few battles it will never feel victorious. Deep down the company knows that it's customers are not happy, and nobody wants unhappy customers.

When new BUSINESS MODELs are being explored it's important to have the guts to consider examples as radical as what happened in the music industry.

Imagine this conversation happening 10 years ago in the Sony Music boardroom? I can, and it's not a happy meeting.

"Why not just give away the very thing we have been selling all these years? In fact, lets make it even easier to give away by streaming on demand to the mobile devices of anyone who wants it."

It's only when you start to explore the impossible, outrageous and just plain stupid ideas that you find a way to get close to what actually might work. Just because you make money selling *widgets* today does not mean you will be in 20, 5 or even 2 years time. Soon you may have to re-think your entire BUSINESS MODEL, so, you may as well get started.

The best place to start thinking about what your service is going to include is to brainstorm some ideas about what *you* might like. If you can't find some things that would get *you* excited about dealing with your company then your customers are not going to find anything either.

GETTING INSPIRED OR... STEALING

RE:DESIGNING your BUSINESS MODEL does not have to be a solo effort. There are no prizes for originality when it comes to BUSINESS MODELs. Not everything has to be your idea, it just has to be you who executes the model best.

Using another company as a starting point for your own ideas is exactly how innovation gets started.

If you have started to hear the rumbles of a big change in your industry then act quickly, find out what is going on, who is doing what, what results they are getting... make a call: *could I do this better?* Just because someone else is having a go, does not mean you should not, in fact maybe the opposite. *Because someone is having a go at changing your industry just proves that there are people out there who think things could and should be done differently.*

Think about how other brands have emerged after the success of Starbucks. Starbucks started a revolution in coffee shops. Serving good coffee in convenient locations was (at least in the UK) a novelty until about ten years ago. Thanks to Starbucks and their BUSINESS MODEL, many other companies jumped into the market. Now we have a thriving independent market of coffee shops as well as a series of large chains. All of these firms followed in the footsteps (although most would claim otherwise) of Starbucks.

If you are in an industry where there does not seem to be anything dramatic happening then this could mean that,

- everyone is totally happy and you and your fellow industry competitors are doing an amazing job (not very likely at all is it) or:
- things are either about to, or need to be, shaken up.

The book *The 22 immutable laws of marketing*, says if you cannot be first to market be first in category.

For example, if you were a selling a fizzy drink, rather than attempt to compete with Coke you'd create a new category of fizzy drink. Maybe it would be an energy drink, like **Red Bull** or maybe it would be designed and marketed as a mixer for cocktails. All are fizzy drinks, but have been positioned into totally different markets.

Many people I have spoken to are put off by the idea of innovating because someone else has already, *'beat them to it'*. The winners are anyone who can create a business that meets the demands and requirements of its customers, make this your aim and there are usually plenty of big opportunities to be found.

It's never very long before industries go through some kind of innovative change, it is your job to make sure you are at the right end of it.

If not much feels like its happening right now, great, set some time aside every month, or if you can every week and start working on your next move. If you don't, then someone else will.

GETTING THE JOB DONE

Most companies end up building a service that keeps most of the people, kind of happy, most of the time. Every customer is different, another *cliché*. That means that your service and offering should be different depending on who your customer is. If you only have the resources to target one kind of customer, then thats who you should target. Pleasing the majority of people can be expensive and unproductive. It means compromising your marketing and sales effort, and most importantly how you deliver your service to each group of customers. No one really gets what they want, instead they get something that is, *'good enough'*.

We have talked about the idea of creating a service for customers that they love so much, they can't help but want to spread the word for you. To do this your business must be focused on *just* doing this. Adding unnecessary features to your *BUSINESS MODEL* can make your service harder to manage and execute and usually result in a compromise your existing customers. The effects of this being that neither get the experience you intend, both are just satisfied and neither rave about you to their friends.

Again, because of how widely known the story and products are, lets look at the Apple range of notebook computers.

They make only two types of notebook, one for the everyday users, a MacBook Air and one for the 'power' user, a MacBook Pro. Each model has a few options for screen size and memory, but even then there are only have 6 choices.

If you were an *on site* construction worker, there are notebook makers who have designed computers with super hard casing, extra bright displays and water proof keyboards for use in a outdoor or dusty environment. On the face of it some of those features would be nice for every laptop (especially for anyone like me who has dropped a notebook on a concrete floor or spilled a glass of wine over a keyboard). The issue is that if Apple included these features in their machines they would need to add weight, reduce battery life etc... they would remove the features that their core customers love.

In fact, this is exactly what happened to Apple in the mid eighties and nineties. Apple released a diverse range of hardware aimed at completely different markets. Ultimately their message to consumers became confused. They were neither in the corporate or the consumer *camp*. Trying to please too many people, left them not really making and impact anywhere. Loosing focus and direction as a company, not knowing who to focus their attention on was almost the end for this now, RE:DESIGNED company. Steve Jobs' contribution to Apple, was that he RE:DESIGNED the BUSINESS MODEL.

Companies like Sony and HP, have fallen way behind Apple in the notebook market and it's clear why sales have fallen off a cliff in the last 5 years. Sony have 19 choices for notebooks, HP who were recently playing with the idea of exiting the hardware market have 22 choices. I have just spent a few minutes looking through their marketing notes online and cannot really understand what the difference is between each model. I know that both Sony and HP ship a large number of notebooks, but they are not really making any money with these devices. Price has become their leading point of difference, and we all know what that means.

What customers want is to have your service do exactly what they need it to do, nothing more and nothing less.

This may at first sound flippant and obvious, but think about it. How often do you buy a service or a product, only to use half of it's capability.

A few years ago I was working with the owner of a business that provided a, personal concierge service. The business was struggling and the owner was on the verge of giving up. About 10 months later after we had changed the model, and got some focus, she actually found someone who loved her business so much that she was able to sell it.

The issue she had was that because she sold a service that could have included, '*anything the client wanted*', she found it hard to market, sell and actually get customers to use. For example, she would offer a birthday gift selection and collection service, a flower delivery service, a shopping service, a travel arrangement service, a car collection service... I could go on. Her job and the job of the people who worked for her was to get things done for people with little time. A great idea.

The challenge was that there was no structure to her day, some weeks she was manic, others she was calling customers to, '*see if they had anything for her to do*'. Customers were kind of happy, but because of the way the business had been marketed most were very low users or even requested one off tasks.

The change came when we RE:DESIGNED the BUSINESS MODEL. Only three service options, a very focused target market, a very clear list of tasks that could be undertaken, easy to understand pricing and maybe most importantly really easy to explain. The types of task that customers we able to request were limited and how clients were able to pay for the services was changed from a "per hour' model to a monthly membership.

This actually meant that the business lost about 70% of it's customers... the great thing was that the ones who stayed more than made up the difference in revenue because they now had a clear picture of how they should use the service. Finally we were able to focus the marketing communication and request for referrals on a highly specific group of people and finding new clients became much more straightforward. It's worth saying that we also developed an online client management tool that gave everyone open access to current client activity from wherever they were (just to tie in with my previous point about technology).

This business was not a huge company. It was a small business. I mention it because I see so many small and medium sized businesses try to over complicate what they do and end up not doing anything truly brilliant. A simple and focused service without gimmicks will always be more attractive to customers and efficient to run over the long term.

Maybe small and medium sized companies need permission to behave like Apple (sorry to keep using Apple, but they really have done some amazing things recently). Well here it is, you have my permission. Go forth and adapt or create a BUSINESS MODEL that is so simple that even a child would understand what you did, and how you did it.

This simple approach focuses on the, *Job to be done*. This means focusing on what the customer wants doing and not on what the *business does*. Nobody wants *dentistry*, they want healthy teeth and gums.

Within every business, even businesses that appear to be in what would seem to be the same industry, the *job to be done* could be dramatically different. A bicycle manufacturer for example could have the *job* of;

- Getting it's customers to the local shop
- Helping it's customers win bike races
- Providing a safe bike for children to learn to ride.

Nobody wants *a bicycle,* they want they can do with it.

Understanding what *Job* your customers need doing is your first step in RE:DESIGNING your BUSINESS MODEL. To do this we always start with people in mind.

It's important to remember that you are in business to provide a service to people. The industry you are in is unimportant. What is important is that there is *someone* or *some-group* of people you are there to serve. When considering the question of, *What job needs doing?*, first look at who these people are.

You could get the best design team in the world to create an amazing BUSINESS MODEL that was interesting and inspiring, but if it did not solve your customers key issues by, *getting there job done,* it would be useless.

The three key questions required to *CALIBRATE* your design process are,

Who needs a job doing?

What job needs doing?

Why do these people need help doing it?

WHAT NEEDS TO BE DONE

CREATE A RE:DESIGN HABBIT

The process of RE:DESIGN is not a one off *task* to be undertaken by a project manager. It's an ongoing process of evaluation, design, adaptation, execution and evaluation *again*.

From time to time it's OK to call in help and outside resources to help you figure out what your next BUSINESS MODEL will look like and even help you implement some of the changes. But the process of re-evaluating your *BUSINESS MODEL* is down to you.

Think of it in the same way as a good diet and exercise. In short sharp bursts more damage can be done than good created. When you start the process, start a habit.

The *RE:DESIGN* tools in this book form the outline of a process that will help you evaluate your model. Although how often you use these tools will depend on the complexity of your company and industry, there are some guidelines.

At the very least your *BUSINESS MODEL* needs evaluating every ninety days. This does not mean that you will make significant changes that regularly. It allows you to remain *in tune* with what is required. It should be treated as business planning exercise, using each review session to evaluate your current results, set new targets for next quarter and create an *Execution Plan*.

For many years I have run similar ninety day planning sessions with clients. On average ninety day intervals seems to be the *Goldilocks period* for evaluation. Longer intervals can mean that critical industry or business developments are left out and, short periods are usually too soon to examine results. In startups, large or complex companies these periods adjust accordingly.

PROTOTYPES, TESTING & LAUNCH

It's important to look at your new BUSINESS MODEL as a prototype for one simple reason. A prototype by definition is not the finished article.

The moment you see your business as finished, something is likely to come along, change the industry or effect the market, and, then your business will have to adapt and change too. The great thing about prototypes is that it's always OK to improve, add another version and even start again when things really are not working.

Its the job of people who run companies to be the designers of this prototype, business designers if you like. Always re-imagining of new ways to increase the value of the service, the usefulness of the product or the design or delivery.

In the case of RE:DESIGNING an existing business you might want to consider setting up your new business in a protected environment. Maybe put it under a different brand or start by releasing it to a few customers. Whatever you do it's really important to carry out intensive testing of your prototype first. Personally I have wasted thousands in launching products before waiting for the test results only to find we missed a important factor in our calculations or design. Be warned, take your time and check, double check and triple check before letting your new system into the *wild*.

On the other hand don't wait too long. I have not personally experienced this because it's not in my nature to wait, but I know lots of people who end up tinkering for so long, that nothing ever gets done.

Bullets and Cannonballs.

When getting ready to launch your new BUSINESS MODEL it's important to stage it's introduction, especially if you already have an existing business. While things move very fast in todays world, do not rush. Take it slow and make sure you introduce your new model in a way that protects what you have already built. A concept I learnt from **Jim Collins**, *fire bullets and then cannonballs*, is how I now explain this.

Fire Bullets and then cannonballs is a concept from Jim's book, Great By Choice. This book like all of Jim's works is based on years and years of research into some of the most successful companies in the world. Based on this analysis he made an important discovery.

Traditional thinking about business suggests that the most innovative companies are ones who end up on top and most successful. Companies that are prepared to take big risks in return for big rewards. In fact Jim's work shows this to be opposite to reality. It's true that many successful companies look like they are risky innovators but in reality only from an outside perspective. In actual fact what might seem like an overnight success is usually the result of well prepared and executed plans that are built on endless tests and re-test of the concept on a much smaller scale. *Fire bullets and then cannonballs* takes its an analogy taken from old war ships. First the attacking ship would fire bullets at it's target to calibrate it's big cannon. The big cannon takes a long time to load, is expensive and could either sink the enemy or miss and land in the water. Bullets can be quickly fired, and are inexpensive and will act as proof that you are on target.

To get more detail on this I recommend reading *Jim's work*.

For now, it's enough to say that fire bullets and then cannonballs means, test a number of strategies on a small and low risk scale to allow you to calibrate. Fine tune and experiment with what works before betting the company on your new idea.

Looking back over the last ten years there are some businesses that many would have said to be impossible to deliver using technology. It's not till someone actually creates an alternative model that new possibilities are created. Simply saying, "*it wont happen to my industry because...*" , is a sure fire way to make sure someone else comes up with the, *next big thing* in your industry.

The way I see it, you can either wait for someone else to find the *"next big thing"*, or start working on creating it. By following some of the guidelines in this book.

HOW YOUR SALES, MARKETING AND DELIVERY NEED TO ADAPT

Lets look at how most products and services have been marketed and sold to us over the years.

1. A company builds a product or designs a service.
2. A bunch of marketing people sit in a room and try to establish what is good about it.
3. Some advertisers come up with some compelling images and text.
4. Sales people spread the word and try to convince people they need to buy.

The key change in recent years is that now the customers get to do most of your marketing for you. The marketing messages are coming from your customers. You no longer directly control what marketing messages are being spread about your company.

GET IT!

Because even though this is a widely written and discussed topic far too many companies still really don't understand what this means.

In a way this has always been the case, but never has a message been so quick to travel round the world. Never has it been so easy to build or destroy a good reputation in business. And maybe most importantly, never has your previous performance, life history, mistakes and successes been documented, stored and opened up to the public.

Most of us have experienced Ebay, or at least understand how it works. As an EBay seller you are rated on your performance by the people who buy from you. This rating is based on how quickly you deliver, the quality of your product (or at least how well it matches the description you give it and, your ability to deal with any issues that arise through the sale.

The point of Ebay is that there is no hiding place. Within a few years the average customer for your business and mine will not buy unless they can quickly and easily find out all about my performance... a bit like a Ebay rating. Everything must be open and transparent and companies who are not willing to share information about how they work, their current performance, quality issues etc will soon be seen as having something to hide.

I have spoken to audiences about this and seen their faces turn from shocked to terrified.

> 'But I cannot tell my customers about our internal quality issues'.

My response to this is, if you don't then someone else will. What would you prefer? It's no longer a case of if this will happen in your industry, but when. Better to have a business designed to cope with such a situation than have this new open culture forced upon you before you are ready.

Because the internet is now so open it's pointless spending time and money on marketing and sales, at least till you have a product or service that kind of sells it's self. I have a friend, David Holland (Founder of Results Rules OK and Author) who said the other day, *'a great products of services does not need to be sold, it needs to be rationed'*.

And that's a huge change in mindset for most businesses.

So there are two important points to consider when looking at how our **BUSINESS MODEL**s will change,

- the world is now much more open. you must now get your customers to do the selling for you by doing a job worth talking about.
- your services must integrate into peoples lives and be more useful than the current standard in your industry.

Take a moment to think about how the atmosphere in your company might change if...

- Everyone knew that the only thing that mattered was that every customer left happy.
- Actually made that happen.

-
- How might the conversations between the team change?
- What would happen to the moral of the team?
- How might this impact on how your customers felt about your business?

I know it's impossible to keep everyone happy all the time, but imagine if you could get even close.

Most companies think that the most important part of what they do is the bit that customers pay for. For example a hairdresser getting paid for cutting hair a builder getting paid for building. In reality customers are paying for the entire experience.

Would you rather get your haircut in a high street barber shop or a luxury spa style salon? There is no right or wrong answer, but it would be reasonable to expect to pay extra for the spa. There is a lot more work involved in delivering a high end haircut in a spa. You may walk away with almost the same haircut, but you'd feel totally different about it.

Some recent research into this topic has gone one step further in proving the point that delivery and experience is far more important than product.

Caltech (California Institute of Technology) produced some research results in 2008 regarding peoples perception of wine. In double bind tests participants were asked to test different wines in unmarked glasses. Each glass was labeled with a price. Some of the prices were correct and others, were not. The experiment was designed to determine what effect the price point and therefore perception of the wine had on how well it was actually enjoyed. Additionally, each participant was wired to a brain scanner that monitored for activity.

The results showed that on average people said they, 'enjoyed' the wines labeled with the highest price tags more, no matter what was in the glass. Furthermore, this was still the case when the wine was labeled with the correct price tag. On the face of it this may seem like the participants we simply using the price label to gage their enjoyment, but there was one other interesting discovery. The brain scans showed a particular part of the brain would, *light up* when participants were drinking the wine they said they '*enjoyed the most*'. This part of the brain, the orbitofrontal cortex, showed the same pattern regardless of whether the participants were drinking cheep plonk or prize winning Bordeaux. The point is that they really did enjoy the wine more. The price actually effected the participants enjoyment of the wine.

You can read more on this study here: http://media.caltech.edu/press_releases/13091

This study helps us understand the effects of how we present and package our services. With the wine the *higher price* indicated that, what was being drunk would be more pleasurable, but it's not just price. In the '*wine world*' price is one of the only things that can highlight a bottle as being, *good*. Most of us have learned, as it turns out incorrectly, that cheap wine is bad wine and expensive wine is good. The price is actually part of the experience. In your industry it might not be price.

If you were in the bakery business maybe one of the things that would add or detract from your customer experience might be the packaging in which you sold your cakes. In the hotel business it could the way your team deal with customers on arrival.

Price can be part of setting your experience but in most businesses there are dozens of other important factors.

The experience and how the service is delivered is much more important than the product its self.

In the same way a hairdresser can standout by creating a luxury environment, a wine producer can sell at a high price or a baker can use fancy packaging. Every business can use technology enabled by the internet to stand out from the competition. Nothing else has the power to simplify and integrate your business with your customers as well as internet enabled technology.

Of course it is far more important to get the real life customer experience working before you even begin to think about how the internet can help. But unless you are working on adding some kind of online integration with your business then very soon you will be left behind, because some other company will be. I can almost guarantee that someone in your industry and probably in your local market is already making moves towards this.

When I work with companies on this challenge I like to think about including the technology enabled services from the very start of designing a new BUSINESS MODEL.

A few weeks ago I was speaking at a conference in London about this subject. The audience were mainly owners of small and medium sized companies. After I got off my *'RE:DESIGN your business'* soap box an audience member said,

> "ah but Chris, what you don't understand is that our customers don't want change. We already tried to deliver our service over the internet and our customers didn't like it...'.

I understand that you might not get all your customers jumping on the band wagon of the changes you make, but this is missing a critical point. It's not that your customers do not want change, it's not that they prefer to see you face to face, we all have enough friends, or even that your business cannot be migrated to a more streamlined technology enabled service. What I believe this lady was actually saying was,

> "I tried to deliver my service to my customers online, and failed because I did not do it very well.".

This might seem brash, but I cannot thing of an industry that will not need to shift its BUSINESS MODEL within the next few years.

If you simply turn off face to face contact with your customers and announce your are now *doing business online* then of course you would expect your customers to be upset. This is not embracing technology. This is mealy abandoning your customers. Your BUSINESS MODEL RE:DESIGN needs to be undertaken with plenty of preparation, planning, evaluation and re-evaluation. The key difference between those who make this work and those who don't is execution.

Like anything worth doing, RE-DESIGING your business will take effort. Don't avoid the effort by simply jumping on the band wagon, like many people did when it came to developing a website. How many businesses do you know that have simply built a website, just because they think they need one? How many of these sites are actually useful? Take sufficient time, follow a clear project plan. Use the tools in this book as a guide.

Every business has the opportunity to use technology to improve their service. I cannot emphasize this enough. The service your customers experience when dealing with your company is the most important part of your business.

Because of the way we all use the internet businesses have now partly lost control of what messages posted about you online. In effect this means being a great company, delivering outstanding service and encouraging people to spread positive messages about you is your "new marketing" strategy.

Delivering great service is now one of the only things you can be sure you will always be able to control.

Just take a look at the history of pretty much any industry to see that very rarely does the best product win, and when it does it's always because the customer service of that company backed up the products. As the song says, *'it ain't what you do, its the way you do it...and thats what gets results'*.

Most businesses have not yet adapted their BUSINESS MODELs. If you can find a way to delivery your product or service in a way that really improves peoples experience and then integrate your marketing into your delivery then you will find it easy to standout and let your customers spread the word for you.

The way you deliver is more important than product or service.

CUSTOMERS IN-CENTIVES FOR CHANGE

There is much talk in the business press about the importance of *building relationships* and your *brand*. Most of these writings talk about these two important topics as if they are, *tasks* to be added to next weeks *to-do list*. These are not activities, they are results of activities.

In business it's common for companies to embark on, *Brand Building* exercises. Why is it in business we tend to over complicate very simple things. Nobody says, I am going on a *relationship building exercise* with a girl I just met! They say I am going on a *date*.

Your business relationships and your *brand*, are overused terms used to establish if anyone actually likes you. If they do you'll have great relationships and a *positive brand image*.

As people, we get other people to like us by being loving, showing appreciation and gratitude, being consistent and helpful.

As businesses we get people to like us by performing well in four categories. 1. Speed and consistency 2. Price 3. Location and accessibility 4. Look and feel.

Working on these areas is where your attention and improvement efforts must lie. Getting more people to *like you* is the results of being better at these four things. The focus some firms put on *Building a brand* or *Creating relationships* seems forced and fake.

A friend of mine says,

> "It's none of your business what other people think about you."

And he is right. There is no need to concern yourself with Brand or Relationships. Just do a great job and these things will come.

SPEED AND CONSISTENCY

How fast you can get your customers what they want and how regularly you deliver on your promises. As a rule of thumb customers want everything in an *instant* and you need to aim to deliver what you promise at least 100% of the time. Easy then!

PRICE

Not necessarily how low your price is, but how well it represents your offering. Sometimes having a price that is too low can put people off!

LOCATION & ACCESSIBILITY

If your business is one where customers visit, how convenient is it to get there. If your business is one where your products and services are accessed remotely, how easy is it to do so.

Two very quick examples here...

THE LOCAL BAKER
A local bakery in my town serves the best bread. It's really easy to get to by foot and while parking

can sometimes be a challenge it's usually not a problem. Not everyone shops there. Why? Because the bakery in the local supermarket is located actually, in the store. It's much more convenient to get bread while getting other shopping too.

PRINTING BUSINESS CARDS
I recently needed to get some business cards printed. I have a local printing shop that is located on my way home form the office. But, I used an online service that just let me order the cards from my desk and have them delivered in a few days. It was just more convenient.

LOOK & FEEL

This is the part the *branding* guys really love.

How well does the look and feel of your business match your intentions for how it should look and feel?

Everything from your company logo and imagery, to the building your business is located in, to the way your people dress and behave at work to the layout and structure of your website.

You may not have the design skills to create these images, but we all have the ability to come up with a concept.

FEATURES OF YOUR NEW BUSINESS MODEL

There are a few really interesting BUSINESS MODEL ideas that have emerged as realistic alternatives over the last ten years. At first they could feel radical. Especially when introduced into a traditional business environment, but, take time to consider how you might include these concepts, if you had to.

These ideas will not be suitable for every industry, business or market, but by exploring the idea of how they could be applied usually leads to some very interesting insights.

FREEMIUM

Here is an interesting question. If you were forced to give away your core products or services how would you make money?

I ask this question because more and more companies are turning to what has become known as a *freemium* model for doing business, especially internet businesses. Is this something that could work in your industry?

Freemium is where a company, lets use Google as an example, gives away it's core solution and makes money else where. In the case of Google it allows us all to use its search engine in return we must look at some adverts that it gets paid for. Another example might be a service we use in my businesses for sending mass emails, mailchimp.com.

mailchimp.com offers a free account with up to 2000 subscribers, if you are a high user then *Mailchimp* starts to charge.

These companies aim to attract large numbers of customers who pay nothing and then make money from the high-end users. This is great because it is so easy to sell a FREE service, it's so attractive to users. I have read lots on this subject and found many people who take the view that this model will not last. Doubters say that by giving away a service for free you de-value it. Another argument is that customers should expect to pay for a good service.

I see it as a great way of marketing and promoting your services. If you do a good job then you will create an army of users who will help spread the word and find you your key customers.

There are of course some risks. Making sure you can cope with demand and understanding your numbers and budgets, but this is also the case for running any business strategy. Consider it as a marketing campaign. How much would you need to invest into generating a new customer? How might this compare to other marketing activities run by your company?

This model is not just for internet businesses. *Vistaprint* is a printing company that gives away business cards. The free versions come with their logo on the back, but you can pay to have this removed. Many people in very small businesses don't bother and there are now hundreds of thousands of business cards floating round the world with the logo and contact details of *Vistaprint*, what a great way to spread the word about your business.

I have also seen this work for a small bakery. A friend of mine was consulting with the owner of a bakery a few years ago and they decided to start giving away their most popular cake, a chocolate eclair. They put an add in the paper, told everyone about it and all of a sudden they had huge lines of people waiting outside their shop everyday waiting to get their free cake. The bakery made back the money in selling other things while the customers collected their cake. Brilliant! The other side effect of this strategy was the word of mouth stories it generated. Everyone wanted to talk about getting a free cake because it's such a good deal. How many people would have talked about the store if they simply found an add in the local newspaper?

You need to fully understand the numbers before getting into something like this and I am not saying this model would work for every business. But if you had to start from this point of view what could you offer? This becomes a great place to start thinking about how your business might look in the future.

ONDEMAND

We have become used to getting what we want when we want it. Think about the last time you made a significant purchasing decision. I bet that 9 times out of 10 you did some research online beforehand

Unless you were searching for a very unusual product or service, you were able to get the information you needed when you wanted it. Not only that, but, you had multiple sources of information. Sales brochures from the company who made the product or service. Reviews from some of their customers. Professional comparisons from industry experts and bloggers and most importantly personal recommendations from your social network (FaceBook, Twitter, LinkedIn etc). But that is just the beginning.

It's no longer enough just to have information about your offering available online. You also have to have a away of interacting with your potential customers quickly and even make part of your services or product instantly deliverable at super fast speed.

I am so used to accessing services at the touch of a button that when I can't get what I want, instantly, I get a little frustrated. Writing this down feels ridiculous but I know I am not alone. I even get frustrated when I have to wait for my latest Amazon order to arrive after ordering, sometimes even 3 days!

What Amazon have done to reduce my frustration is let me pickup the phone anytime day or night and call someone at the Amazon Service Centre and ask about my order. They have given me *ON DEMAND*, instant access.

Have you ever started to search for a company to help with something and skipped the first few webpages that don't seem to be able to provide you with a quick online quote or give you instant access? I bet you have, at least statistics say you have. Depending on what you read the average bounce rate (percentage of visitors that leave your website after seeing the first page) is between 45% and 65%. This means that about half the people who get to your site, can't find what they are looking for within the first few seconds.

Some companies spend thousands on building websites that look great but fail at the stage of actually getting the important information to the potential customer. Instead they cop out and put a banner that says, *call us now for a quote*.

When there really is no other option this can be fine, but really it should be a last measure. You absolutely must have some kind of *'call to action'*, it's just you should do better than, *Call us for a Quote*. When I ask audiences the question, how many people here when searching the web skip to another website when they see a, *call us now for a quote*, banner, about 70% of the people in the room raise their hand. Yet, when I ask the question, how many people have this remark or something similar on their own website about 90% of the room admits it. The thing is that *knowing* this and *doing* something about it are very different things.

There is a very real counter argument that says if you hold back info and get people to call, then you can start to build a relationship over the phone, bring them into your sales system, make sure they understand all the features and benefits... basically, sell them more stuff. This could be true, but does the process really have the customers best interests at its heart? I think not. Nobody likes to be sold to. This is a pattern that is playing out across almost every industry I can think of. This is about making your product/service something that people buy, not something that is sold. You still need great customer service people to help support the buying process but that is all they are doing, supporting the process.

Consumers are moving towards companies who put them in full control and make their service or product available where and when it's required. *ONDEMAND* BUSINESS MODELs focus on removing the hurdles customers must go though to purchase and get what they want.

MOBILE

There is a big focus right now on mobile applications and on businesses that embrace mobile technology. This is going to be very important but the most interesting thing is why.

Making applications available to use on the move massively improves usefulness. Most of us now carry a device that can access the internet on the move and so it enables businesses to put their services *literally* in the hands of its customers. Until recently most of the services we were able to access from mobile devices were mainly information based (google searches, weather and news reports etc), now we are seeing more and more emerging services that allow interaction, processing and completion of tasks.

I, and many others have managed to almost abandon my notebook and desktop computer in favor of my iPad and iPhone. Many of the businesses I buy from have integrated their services with mobile-internet enabled technology. This means we can now actually, *get stuff done*, while away from the office. It used to be that I would use my mobile phone as a kind of task list. I would use it to remind me to do things when I got back to the office, now I am actually getting things done while on the move.

We recently ran an event with the American author and speaker, *Jim Collins*. The whole booking system including, marketing, ticket confirmation and payment collection, presentation creation and even supplier payment was done using apps on the iPhone. Much of the process was automated but a great deal of tasks that I would usually have to deal with from my desk I actually completed while traveling. I am not quite ready to give up my notebook, but I am getting there.

Right now the biggest investments by private equity firms is in technology companies that integrate mobile services. The reason is, that mobile internet speeds are now fast enough to actually deliver useful services to users on the move.

This means, when looking at RE:DESIGNING your BUSINESS MODEL, considering how people want to access it is one of the highest priorities. It does not necessarily mean you have to make your product deliverable to remote users. It does mean you should consider giving them access to key information and the most important features of your service wherever they are.

A great example of how mobile technology is being used with an every day business is the BUSINESS MODEL developed by HailOcab.com.

This is a great application for taxi firms. The app will let you book a cab in with two clicks, it then sends your current location to the nearest available taxi and reports back to you its current location and exact time of arrival. Why would you ever telephone a cab again?

Your *mobile* integration could be even more simple. One of my clients is an on demand manufacturing firm who make electronic components. Sometimes their customers need to know exactly what they have in stock, in production and on order while they are out of the office or away from their desk. We have build a simple reporting tool that allows them to remotely login and see a live report of *whats going on with their account*.

All these additions are not really *what the customer is paying for*, or at least if you asked the customers of these companies what they were paying for it's unlikely they would mention the features above. If asked most people would say they were paying for the *taxi ride* or the *cable assembly*. The reality is the experience of buying the product/service and how it's delivered is a significant part of the buying decision. This also means it's a significant part of the cost of delivery, yet many or even most small and medium size companies spend little resources getting this bit right.

I have had many conversations with business owners who are looking for more products and services to add to their offering in a hope to boost revenues and reach a wider market. In most cases it's not what your company does, but how it does it, that will have the biggest impact.

These features can become the most important element of your BUSINESS MODEL. They are the things that when done well, make the business stand out above the competition. If you were choosing to do business with a new supplier, and everything else was the same except some kind of *on demand or mobile* feature as described above, who would you do business with?

Not having these additional features as part of your offering within a few years may even make it hard to continue in business, at least till you have sorted it out.

Having *On Demand* and *Mobile* features as part of your BUSINESS MODEL is about getting the important information to your customer and potential customers where and when they need it. This might be just getting them pricing and delivery options with a buy now button or it could be delivering the whole product or service directly over the internet. The key thing is that your customer is getting what they want, where they want it and when they want it.

Who can argue that this is not a good option to offer?

SOCIAL & COMMUNITY

Social enterprises and community led Co-Ops are in vogue. Pickup any business related journal and you are bound to discover a few articles about how *selfless entrepreneurs* have given up their dreams of riches in favor of saving the planet, or some other nobel cause.

Huh, I just read that back and realised how pessimistic it must sound. It's not meant to be.

The issue I take with focusing on setting up *social enterprises* is that it implies that making a personal profit is in essence, wrong. Let's be clear, it's OK to get rich from creating a great business.

Businesses that fail to support their community and *do good* in the world will find life harder and harder. This is mainly due to our new COMMUNICATION 3.0 standard discussed earlier in this book.

I know there are still some enormous corporations that operate in a way that really does not add any good to our world, but I can assure you they are either quickly changing or leaving us for good.

As our communication improves there will be no way any business can operate in a way it would rather the world did not know about. The world will find out. Think of the people of the world as a kind of, open source regulation board. Do a bad thing and everyone will know what you did.

Aiming to be a *Social Enterprise* is great, but actually *every* business needs to make sure their model supports local community. *Social Enterprise* is sometimes an excuse for not making any money. Having shareholders who demand a profit keeps businesses efficient.

This does not mean that the idea of giving all your profits back to the community as a charitable donation is a bad idea. Labeling your business as a *Social Enterprise,* at least in my mind is confusing.

I would much rather a business be run as a business and make a profit. Then if you choose to give a donation to your local community you can.

I find a much more targeted way to approach this is to set, donation goals. This year we are giving away £1,000,000 to our local schools. Then go and build a business that is efficient enough to give away your promised donation.

If you choose to give away your profits or not you had better make sure your business is supportive and helpful. I can't imagine anyone not wishing this to be the case, but now it's important to ensure you are delivering.

END TO END

Is it possible for me to include one more example regarding Apple? It's my book, I will do what I want.

Do you remember the Diamond RIO? or the Creative Zen? I owned a Sony MW-MS70D (great name I know). My guess is that you don't remember these early MP3 music players. Obviously the one we do remember is the one we are using eleven years after it's launch, the iPod.

So what made the iPod better than the dozens of other MP3 players that entered the market between 2001 and 2004?

The iPod was not a standalone product. You were not buying an MP3 player, you were buying an *End to End* service. Yes you got the MP3 music player and the iconic white earbuds, but what got people actually using the music player was how simple it was to use.

It was the first MP3 player that integrated with an *Online Music store*. As a user you could (in fact you still can), plug in your device, select a few songs from the *iTunes Store* and in a few minutes you'd be ready to go.

In comparison, my Sony MP3 player had the same 50 songs loaded for at least 8 months, just because it was such a pain to load a new playlist.

So how does this help us when building our BUSINESS MODELs?

Apple focused on getting the *job done*. Other players in the MP3 market focused on creating an MP3 player. In fact my Sony player was lighter, sounded great, had long battery life and in many ways actually performed better that an iPod. But it did not actually *do the job* I needed it to do very well.

Apple managed to create an *ecosystem* where their product could perform. In many small and medium sized business it's the services that surround our core offering that are not performing rather than the core service or product itself.

On a recent business trip to Lima, Peru, I found another example of an *End to End* BUSINESS MODEL, that surprised me. Like many developing cities, Lima has a growing number of people interested in health and fitness. One of the challenges in such big congested cities is that there are very few places to put on your running shoes and go for a jog.

To solve this issue a few large sports companies including, **Poweraid** and **Adidas** teamed up to transform a large outdoor park right in the centre of one of Limas up and coming districts into an outdoor fitness centre. The park contains a five kilometer running track, workout equipment, outdoor areas for group classes including yoga, dance and aerobics. The companies that support this project obviously get the advantage of also being able to sell their goods and advertise their products around the park.

I have never seen so many people in one place exercising.

By supporting these projects these companies have created a new *ecosystem* in which people now have the facility to use their products. Now people will buy new training shoes or energy drinks, because they have a environment to make use these things. An *End to End* ecosystem has been created.

One final example. There is a small pub in the town I grew up, Cwmbran, South Wales that is located in a spot that is very difficult to walk to. Although this pub is less than half a mile from a large group of houses, it's down a long, dark and narrow lane, with no sidewalk and lots of fast cars. The owners of the pub have created a free taxi service for customers.

When looking at your BUSINESS MODEL RE:DESIGN consider how your customers will use the service. It might not always be what your are *doing* or *not doing* internally that impacts your business the most. How can you help remove the hurdles customers go through when buying from you.

THE RE:DESIGN PROCESS

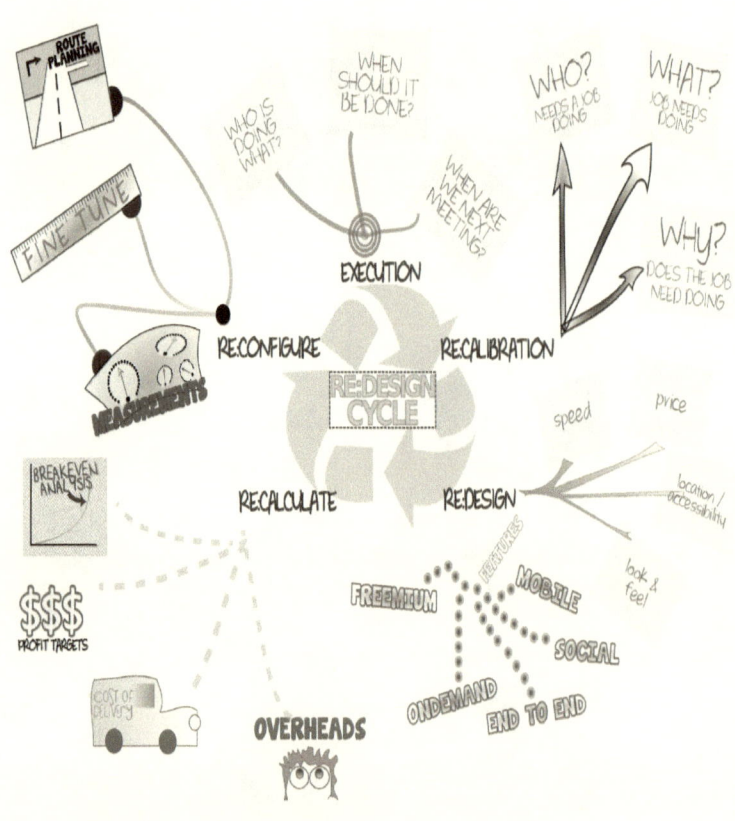

If you have reached this point then it's for one of two reasons,

1) You read the previous chapters and decided to take some action.
2) You already knew it was time to, RE:DESIGN your BUSINESS MODEL and just want to get started.

Either way, welcome to the part of the book that requires your interaction. A kind of *Book 3.0*. If that does not make sense then you should *really* go back and read the previous chapters.

RE:DESIGN CYCLE.

EXECUTION

RE:CONFIGURE RE:CALIBRATION

RE:DESIGN CYCLE

RE:CALCULATE RE:DESIGN

RE:CALIBRATE

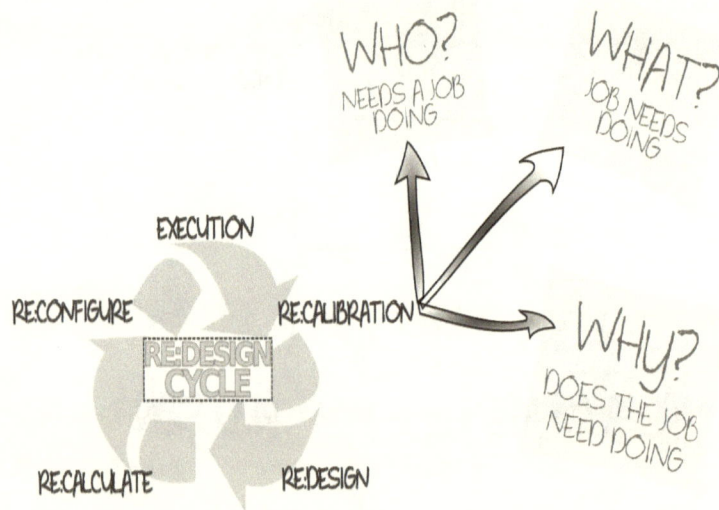

To *Calibrate:* carefully assess, set, or adjust something abstract.

NOTE: Thanks to everyone who has pointed out that *recalibrate* means to *calibrate again*. But I am claiming artistic license with some of these words.

Your business is an abstract entity until it actually performs exactly as you plan it. RE:CALIBRATION is about defining at the purpose of your business.

Have you ever found a product of service that you thought was a great idea, but could not think of who would use, how they would us it or why? Often you see these products being sold on, *homeshopping tv* or at demonstration stands in shopping centers.

Without clearly *calibrating* your *BUSINESS MODEL* runs the risk of creating a marvelously designed service of product that does not actually fulfill a need.

WHO NEEDS A JOB DOING?

The more specific the better. If you are setting up a *Dog Food* business, *WHO,* you need more focus than, *dog owners*. Start by choosing a small niche group, for example, *the owners of dogs for the blind*. It's only when we get specfic that we can start to clearly understand the next question, *What job needs doing?*

WHAT JOB NEEDS DOING?

So now we have a group of people in mind, we start to explore how we can help them get a *job done*. Obviously the kind of *jobs* you focus on will be *within your field of knowledge*. There is little point in aiming to: *help your customers capture memorable images* if you are a butcher or *find and prepare local organic meat,* if you are a photographer. But, then again, who am I to tell you what to do.

WHY DOES THE JOB NEED DOING?

Why the job needs doing, is perhaps the most important part of your RE:CALIBRATION. The *why*, acts a check point to establish if you can be useful to your customers.

If the group of people you wanted to help were; *people who worked from home offices* and the job you wanted to help with was, *sending reliable fax messages*, then when you start evaluating the *why,* you'll find it hard to find a compelling reason.

Why the job needs doing, means establishing motive for your customers to engage your services.

CALIBRATION EXAMPLES:

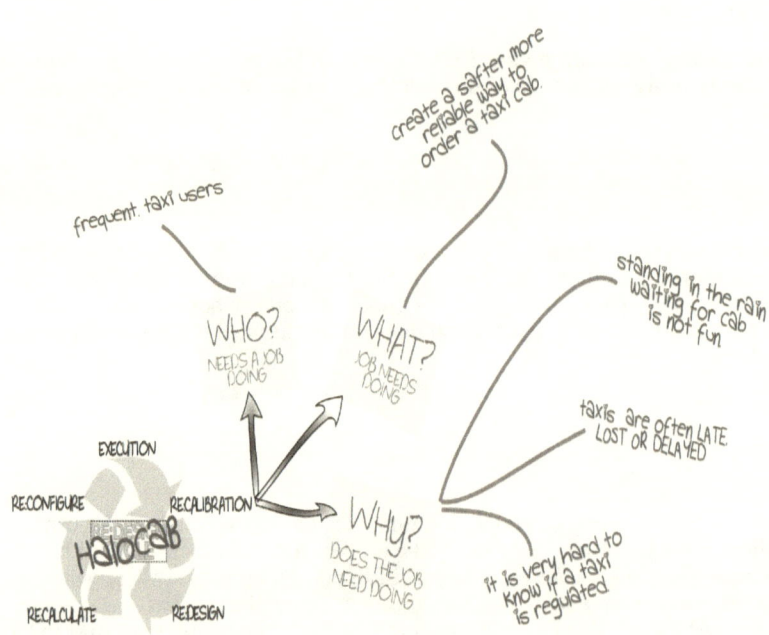

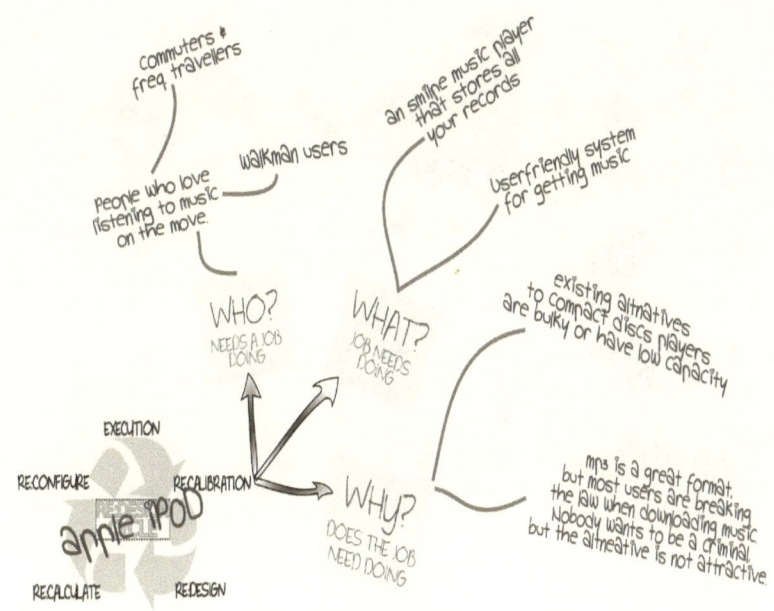

RE:DESIGN

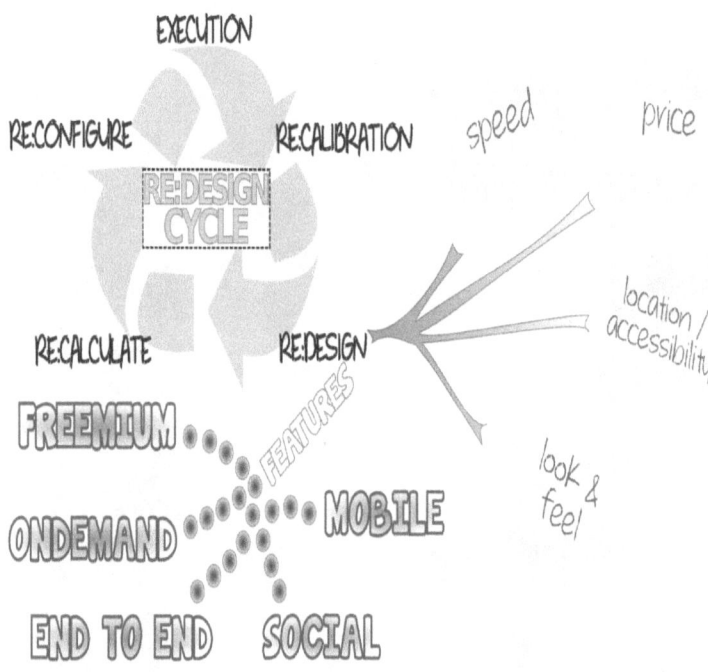

This step is where we get creative and begin imagining some solutions and ideas. This part of the process may take some time but should be a whole lot of fun.

Using the information gathered from your RE:CALIBRATION you can explore how your products and services will *get the job done*, better than what is currently available.

The first four headings, *Speed, Price, Location/Accessibility and Look & Feel*, are for you to define what standards your new BUSINESS MODEL must achieve to meet the requirements of your audience. You are not aiming to define your exact price or look and feel at this point, this will come later. Here your aim to define *what* these areas will achieve.

For example, Ryanair or South West airlines are low cost carriers. Their main attraction is that they are low cost. So it's a requirement that the *Price* element of their BUSINESS MODEL aims to achieve the *lowest prices*. Royles Royce Automobiles is a high-end luxury brand, the *look & feel* therefore must match this image.

The FEATURES arm of RE:DESIGN is a starting point to start working out what features your business might include. Explore each of the options and any other that come to mind for the purpose of brainstorming. By finding solutions to include each feature you are more likely to discover one that stands out. Your final BUSINESS MODEL, could include a combination of more than one feature.

Start the process of exploring each *feature* with the question;

> If our BUSINESS MODEL had to be... , how would we do it?

There is a section on each of these *features* in the pervious section of this book, but I recommend doing your own research on each. You'll find plenty of examples to use as inspiration online.

DESIGN EXAMPLES

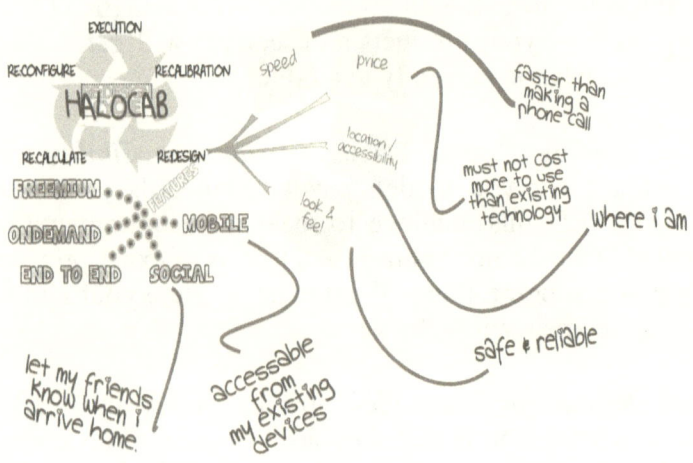

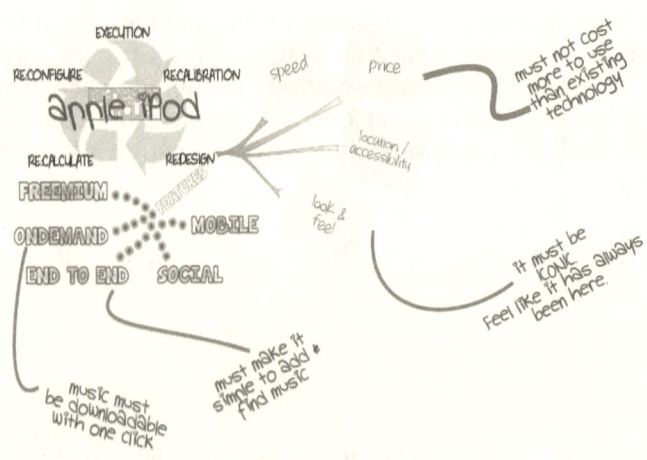

RE:CALCULATE

EXECUTION

RE:CONFIGURE   RE:CALIBRATION

RE:DESIGN CYCLE

RE:CALCULATE   RE:DESIGN

BREAKEVEN ANALYSIS

$$$ PROFIT TARGETS

COST OF DELIVERY

OVERHEADS

Ok once you have an outline for a solution it's time to work out how realistically it could be executed. Creating a fancy concept for your BUSINESS MODEL is nice, but it must be feasible. This section is about working out the basic numbers required to make your BUSINESS MODEL perform.

OVERHEADS

Costs incurred in the general upkeep or running of a plant, premises, or business, and not attributable to specific products or items.

This means adding up all our the expenses you'd face to keep your business alive even if it produced no products of delivered any service. We are talking about items such as office rent, telephone bills, legal and accounting fees, salaries of team not associated with delivery. Because every BUSINESS MODEL, has a different set of *Overheads* you'll need to establish these figures individually.

COST OF DELIVERY

The direct cost associated with delivering specific products or services.

Cost of Delivery (sometimes referred to as, *Direct costs or cost of goods)* are the expenses you only incur when someone buys your product of service. A taxi firm would only purchase fuel if it was giving a customer a ride, a printing firm only purchases paper to print for it's customers.

Defining your *Cost of delivery*, can become tricky in some businesses. For example; the price I pay the printer per book will drop up to 50% per book when I print over 10,000 copies. There is no simple way to define your *cost of delivery* at this stage.

This is why the RE:DESIGN CYCLE is a *cycle,* you will have to go round the *cycle* a few times to tie all the sections together.

Your ultimate aim is to produce a *margin* you can apply to revenue. Your *margin* the the percentage of your revenue remaining after you have paid for *costs of delivery.*

PROFIT TARGETS & BREAK EVEN

How much money you'd like to make.

Most business plans produce their *break even* numbers without including profit. By definition this kind of makes sense, but in the real world it sucks. As an investor or an owner of a business your money is tired up, or in the case of many owners, your time and money is tied up in the business. It's very common for business owners to not even take a salary for their time, on the basis they will, *take it out of profits.*

If you time or money is tied up then it's *not working* else where, meaning there is a hidden cost. You money could be in the bank earning a basic level on interest or your could be working for company that actually paid a salary. Without this your business cannot be certain about when it truly breakeven.

A few years ago I was looking at this issues with a client. She ran a print and design firm with her partner that was making them both a combine income of around, £80,000 per year. The issues was that while running this small business she had been offered salaried positions with other firms that paid as much as £150,000 per year. So in effect her business was costing £70,000 per year. Understanding this she increased her targets to include her lost income.

BREAK EVEN CALCULATION

How much revenue is required to achieve your *Profit Targets*.

(OVERHEADS + PROFIT TARGETS) / MARGIN = BREAK EVEN

RE:CONFIGURE

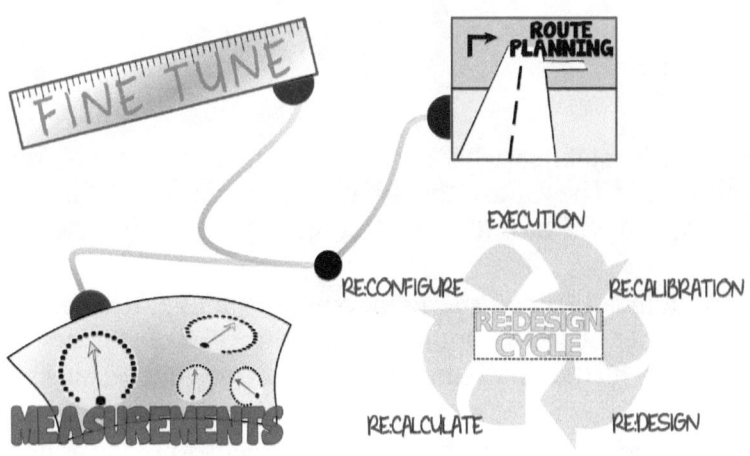

> CONFIGURE: shape or put together in a particular form.

Now you have an outline for your BUSINESS MODEL it's time to draw a *map* of how you intend to get there.

MEASUREMENTS

Here you'll establish what critical areas of your business require monitoring. Theses are the areas of your business that matter the most and will have the greatest impact on it's success.

It will included some generic measurements like, Revenue, margins, number of sales enquiries and number of customers, but it should also include measurements specific to your business.

As an *overnight* delivery firm, FedEx's needs to monitor how often it achieves an, *overnight delivery*. As a low cost grocery business, WallMart measures how it's prices compare to the competition. Your business will have it's own key numbers that it must measure to effectively evaluate it's performance.

> FINE-TUNE: make small adjustments to (something) in order to achieve the best or a desired performance.

The previous stages in the RE:DESIGN CYCLE have been mainly abstract. Meaning that they are likely to require adjustments and tweaks before you able to create an effective *plan for action*. In designing your *BUSINESS MODEL* you may visit this section several times, before you have enough clarity.

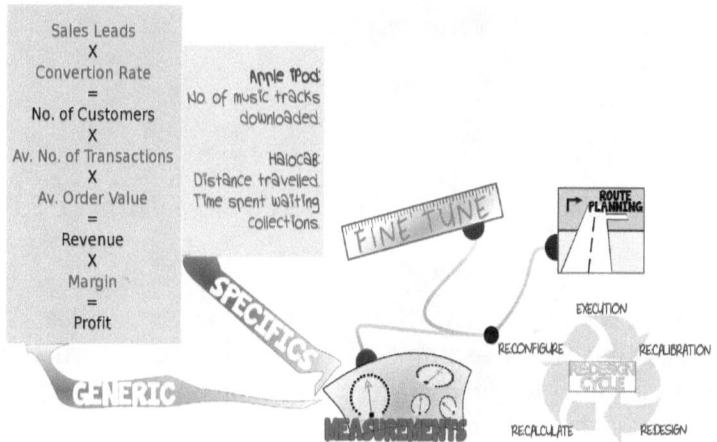

You'll know that it is time to move on to actually creating a *Route Map*, when all the previous sections seems to *tie up* and *make sense*. Do each of the previous sections *flow* or are there still some areas that require more detail of clarity.

The expression, *getting all your ducks in a row*, works well here. *Fine Tuning*, is where you re-evaluate the previous sections and make sure everything is *lined up*.

> ROUTE PLANNING: Working out how you are going to get there.

The penultimate stage of designing your *BUSINESS MODEL* is perhaps the most time consuming. It's where you'll take the details from the previous sections and create a detailed explanation of how you intend to get there.

To gather enough details this section will require many hours of investigation, research and evaluation. Think of it as writing the instruction manual for reaching your targets.

If you have ever built *flat pack* furniture you will have an idea of what's required here. If your *goal* was to build flat pack wardrobe then it would be fairly difficult if the instructions said;

- Assembly draws.
- Build sides.
- Screw everything together...

... yet many business plans often resemble such basic instructions.

Use your own judgement to decide what needs detail and what can be assumed. for example, *flat pack* furniture instructions do not tell you how to, *hold a screwdriver* or how to, *bang a hammer,* they just say *what to screw or hammer where*.

EXECUTION

WHO IS DOING WHAT?

WHEN SHOULD IT BE DONE?

WHEN ARE WE NEXT MEETING?

EXECUTION

RE:CONFIGURE

RE:CALIBRATION

RE:DESIGN CYCLE

RE:CALCULATE

RE:DESIGN

There is one final step. Thats, actually getting going and managing your project. Rather than create your plan, circulate it round the *important people* in your company and then stick it on the shelf (what usually happens), it should be a working document.

From your plan you'll be able to establish a list of priorities, set some time frames and workout, who is going to *do what*.

The final stage is to decide when you are next going to evaluate your plan. Set this time now, decide who will need to be involved and put the time in your calendar. More than anything else, setting this time up now will transform your *BUSINESS MODEL RE:DESIGN* into something that actually gets done, rather than an *good idea*.

Keep these design and planning meeting going requires discipline but is a powerful tool to keep your business and the people focused on the right things.

It's just the beginning

The RE:DESIGN CYCLE should be used as a brainstorming tool. It's designed to help you construct the key building blocks of your plan, not actually *be your plan*. Think of a completed RE:DESIGN CYCLE as page one of your plan, your *table of contents*.

After you complete each section you'll need to plan out the details of exactly how you intend to achieve it.

As the name suggests the RE:DESIGN CYCLE is a *cycle*. It's not a one off activity to perform at your next *team building day* (although working on this with your team is critical). The RE;DESIGN CYCLE is an ongoing *BUSINESS MODELing and Planning* strategy. Built into the RE:DESIGN CYCLE is, *Analysis & Evaluation, Creative Brainstorming, Technical & Financial feasibility and Management and Execution.* Or to put it simply, it will help you figure out;

- What you are going to do
- How you are going to do
- Keep you on track for getting it done.
·

Have you ever created a *planning document* that actually just ended it's life sat on a shelf? You would not be alone if you had. The key to building a great planning document is making it a *tool* rather than an instruction manual. It should focus on the *activities* you need to accomplish rather than the results you'd like to achieve.

In my line of work it's not uncommon for me to have dozens of *Business Plans* on my desk at anyone time. The most frustrating *Business Plans,* spend far too much time explaining, *What they are going to do,* and almost no time explaining, *how they are going to do*. *What* you are going to do is important, but without a clearly outlined *plan* stating how you intend to get there, you are unlikely to leave the *starting blocks*.

The *RE:DESIGN CYCLE* focuses your attention on, *what you are going to do*, and only touches on the basics of, *how you are going to do it*. After running through the tool you will need to expand each section to explain the details of how you intend to achieve your plan.

I have always found that starting business design projects are best done in groups. Even better when the group of people are totally disconnected from your industry and you. This way you are more likely to get new and creative ideas plus some honest feedback to your current BUSINESS MODEL. If all you have available is yourself or your existing team, then of course give the process a go. If you can however, join a group. To make this easier there is a section on our website that will help you setup a group or join an existing group. www.chrisgibbons.net.

Should you choose not to join one of our group sessions then here are some of our keys tips for running a successful RE:DESIGN session.

- GROUPS WORK BEST!
- YOUR GROUP MUST HAVE A FACILITATOR. CHOOSE WISELY!
- CLASSROOM RULES APPLY. – NO SPEAKING OVER OTHER PEOPLE. WAITING YOUR TURN YOU KNOW THE REST.
- 100% PARTICIPATION IS REQUIRED
- GET OUT OF YOUR USUAL ENVIRONMENT – GO SOMEWHERE INSPIRING AND HAVE FUN!

THINGS YOU MAY NEED...

- COLORED MARKERS.
- POST IT NOTES.
- PLAYDO. & LEGO.
- WHITE BOARDS.
- CARDBOARD BOXES.. STRING.. SCISSORS
- MAGAZINES.. NEWSPAPERS
- CAMERAS.. IPADS. PROJECTORS
- PENTLY of WATER. FRUIT. TEA AND COFFEE.

AT LEAST TWO FULL DAYS:

DAY 1: ESTABLISH THE CONCEPT. COMPLETE ALL STAGES. AIM TO PRODUCE AT LEAST TWENTY DIFFERENT SOLUTIONS * * *.

DAY 2: REVIEW AND REFINE YOUR TEN IDEAS. FIND THREE WORKABLE SOLUTIONS. THEN CHOOSE ONE TO EXECUTE.

* * * You may not reach twenty solutions, but push for it. At this point we are aiming for quantity not quality. Forget thinking caps, think playtime.

One final request... please let us know how you get on with your RE-DESIGN.

ABOUT CHRIS

This is my 10th year in the world of business and executive coaching, I can tick most of the boxes when it comes to professional experience - I have either personally coached or trained more than 2,000 senior executives & company directors.

Being a coach is more than job, it's who I am.

I started in the coaching business at the age of 21 with huge goals and ambitions. It was not long before people were lining up to tell me how, 'it was never going to happen for me' or 'why not set you sights a little lower'... I am sure you have had plenty of similar encounters.

At 25 I was feeling pretty smug. Driving fast cars, traveling round the world on business, speaking on stage to thousands of people each year... on the outside things looked good. Of course I was really not that happy. A

 few years later and with the help of some amazing coaching, I started to discover what went wrong for me. It was actually quite simple.

With the right knowledge and action extremely fast results are easily possible... it's my mission to help people get everything they ever wanted.

I have lived in Germany for about 12 months. My partner and I decided we wanted to spend more time with her family while bringing up out little boy, Max. We travel to the UK where I am from about once every 6 weeks to see my family, our friends and to visit some clients.

I started dabbling with business ideas from the age of about 19. Thats if you discount the over used stories of so called Entrepreneurs being in business from the age of 10, because they cut grass or cleaned the car or delivered papers for a few neighbors - I did all those things, but so did all my friends... lets be clear, this does not count as business experience.

I became self-employed at 18 when I joined a company that sold energy utilities. My job was to encourage people to allow my company to bill for your gas, electricity, telephone services etc. I had been selling for about 18 months in some other positions and discovered I quite enjoyed it and that maybe going out on my own would be a good idea. After about 6 weeks of giving it ago, signing up my Mum, next door neighbour and a guy I later found out to be mentally disabled, I was offered a similar position in a bigger company as part of what they called the "*flying in squad*"... honestly one of the main reasons I wanted the job was because it sounded so cool to be part of a *flying in squad!* The idea was we, being *highly trained sales professionals (honestly looking back this makes me cringe, since I now realise that highly skilled was more than an slight overstatement),* would travel round the country giving local under performing sales regions a boost.. The fact I was not yet a very good sales person did not seem to bother the interviewer. Looking back I think the reason I was hired was that I had a car and was able to transport some of the other more experienced sales guys round.

It was doing this job that started me on the path to learning about sales marketing and business. Many of my friends were at university and I saw this as an alternative education. While working in this job I also made a very good income. I remember one of the first weeks where I hit my sales target getting my pay slip (in fact I still have it) for over £1200, this was for one week! When I was 18. To put this in perspective, most of my friends at the time would be lucky to earn half that in a month. One thing I did not learn at this stage was money management, as soon as it came in it went out. I lived away from home in hotels, went out every night, spent about 50% of my time in the pub since I usually completed my sales target by Wednesday the rest of the week was available for fun and games, or just drinking. It was lots of fun and looking back I realise how much I learnt.

Then came the cold winters. It's not fun knocking on doors in the winter. I decided to get an office job, one where I could learn more about business.

The first job I found was for an office administrator, with a firm of Business Coaches. The whole idea of business coaching was foreign to me (and most other people at the time), it was 2002 and this was the launch of a UK office of an Australian company. To be totally honest even after the interview I still had no idea what Business Coaching was, what my role would be, or who the boss was.

Anyway I got the job, met some brilliant people, saw some clients get great results and eventually progressed through the ranks to eventually setup my own Business Coaching firm.

Apart from that I spend my time contributing to The Business Journal Online (a business publication I co-founded with The Times journalist, Daniel J Lloyd), coaching a small number of businesses and when the opportunities arise speaking at workshops and events about the subject in this book.

If you want to keep up with what I'm working on have a look at my website, chrisgibbons.net.

RESOURCES & RECOMMENDATIONS FOR INSPIRATION ON CUSTOMER EXPERIENCE RE:DESIGN

As I have already explained, this book is not really about giving you a lesson in customer service. I do hope it's a catalysis for getting started on designing your next BUSINESS MODEL.

Some of the most valuable books I have read on this subject are...

Delivering Happiness - Tony Hsieh
Screw business as usual - Sir Richard Branson
21 Immutable Laws of marketing - Al Ries and Jack Trout
Your Business Rules OK - David Holland
Sales Bible - Jeffery Gitomer
Buying Customers – Brad Sugars

www.ingramcontent.com/pod-product-compliance
Lightning Source LLC
Chambersburg PA
CBHW021959170526
45157CB00003B/1067